THE
GOOGLE ADWORDS SURVIVAL GUIDE

HOW TO KEEP YOUR HEAD ABOVE WATER, OUTSMART YOUR COMPETITORS, PREVENT BLEEDING BUDGET AND GROW YOUR LOCAL BUSINESS WITH GOOGLE ADWORDS

STEVETENERIELLO

ANCHOR HOUSE MEDIA

AnchorHouseMedia.com

Sales and Service Media Group, Inc.

Published by: Sales & Service Media Group, Inc., Anchor House Media, Boston, Massachusetts
Author: Steve Teneriello
Cover Design & Artwork: Julia Donigian
Production and Composition: Matthew Mazzari

Anchor House Media
PO Box 462
Amesbury, MA 01913
Or online at: www.anchorhousemedia.com

Copyright Submitted to Library of Congress Cataloging-in-Publication Data

Teneriello, Steven, 1982-
        The Google AdWords survival guide: how to keep your head above water, outsmart your competitors, prevent bleeding budgets and grow your local business with Google AdWords/by Steve Teneriello
        p. cm.
Includes bibliographical references.
ISBN-13: 978-0692347805
ISBN-10: 0692347801

*For the lady in my life who makes what I do possible,
my wife Allison, and the little one who inspires me, my
beautiful daughter, Madeline Rose.*

Acknowledgements

I am thankful for all of the people who have helped me get to where I am today:

To my parents who taught me to believe that anything is possible with hard work, commitment and follow-through.

To my clients for trusting in me and giving me an opportunity to earn their ongoing business.

To my editor Matt Mazzari who tied everything together and brought this book to life.

To my incredibly talented graphic designer Julia, who helped turn my vision of this book into a reality from cover to cover.

To my talented management team: James Nagle, Julia Donigian, Matt Mazzari and Tommy Dunn who made this project a reality.

To the teachers, influencers and motivators who have inspired me and have had an impact in shaping my career: Mark Kaplan, Jim Lutz, Greg Peach, Chris Chapman, Paul Mandragouras, Mark Kushinksky, Derek Gilmore, Lee Milteer, Dan Kennedy, Bill Glazer, John Carlton, Dave Dee and Perry Marshall. Thank you.

BONUS RESOURCES FOR THE GOOGLE ADWORDS SURVIVAL GUIDE

Gain access to over $805 worth of money making Google AdWords tools, step-by-step blueprints, and online training.

Discover how you can outsmart your competitors, prevent bleeding budgets, and grow your business with the power of Google AdWords when you join Pay-Per-Click Prosperity – the place for better Google AdWords advertising performance.

Here You'll Gain Access To:

- **Steve's AdWords Survival Blueprint ($29 value):** This one pager will be your best friend when you are attempting to navigate the waters of Google AdWords. It includes Google AdWords vocabulary, The Anatomy of a winning Google AdWords campaign and The Basic Survival Rules in Making Google AdWords work for you.

- **How To Hire a Google AdWords Advertising Manager Worksheet ($97 value):** This comprehensive worksheet includes the 21 essential interview questions you need to ask AdWords manager candidates to see if they are qualified to manage your precious advertising budget.

- **5 Step-By-Step Ways To Capture More Opportunities Using The Right Technology Webinar ($297 value):** Register now and watch this pre-recorded webinar on-demand. *Setting The Foundation For Google AdWords Success.* Watching this webinar will give you a clear picture and understanding into how wasted advertising spend can be easily be avoided, how you'll generate more leads and how you can implement a competitive edge that will take your competitors by complete surprise.

- **Steve's Ad Copy Survival Blueprint ($97 value):** This is the actual tool Steve uses with clients to develop a go-to market strategy for each and every single campaign he manages. This tool will make sure you don't miss a thing when you begin to craft your ad copy for Google AdWords.

- **Ad Copy Worksheet ($97 value):** This simple and powerful one page worksheet gives you the ability to simulate and test your ad copy. It will tell you exactly how many characters you can fit into your ad. In addition it will provide you with an example on how it will appear on Google's search results page.

- **Steve's Landing Page Survival Cheat Sheet ($29 value):** This guide provides you with all of the built-in best practices you should incorporate into your landing pages. Following these 10 essential landing page tips will keep your pages converting again and again.

- **3 Legged Stool of AdWords Success Worksheet ($47 value):** Built with more than 20 business metrics, this simple and easy tool will help you figure out how many leads your organization needs and how much you should budget for when launching a Google AdWords campaign. You will see directly how slight improvements in PPC management, call center management and sales management can impact revenue with this smart tool.

- **The Pay-Per-Click Scorecard ($97 value):** This powerful management template gives you the ability to measure and track the 14 key performance metrics that impact your Google AdWords return on investment. You'll be able to track all of your core AdWords, call center and revenue performance and tie it back to your monthly budget. This tool allows you to collect data month over month so you can keep a pulse on your month-over-month averages.

- **Free 30-Minute Review of your Google AdWords Account** Along with action items you can take to make immediate improvements with an experienced PPC lead generation and conversion specialist on Steve's team.

- **Free 30-Day Trial to ClickOptix Conversion Optimization and Reporting Software:** Never feel lost again with access to our real-time business reporting software – ClickOptix. You'll have up-to-the-minute access to the health, well-being, and critical reporting metrics that make your phone ring. View clicks, conversion rates, calls, top performing keywords, click fraud and much more.

- **Monthly Newsletter:** Stay up-to-date with changes, news and events and receive the monthly Pay-Per-Click Prosperity Client-Only Newsletter.

- **Weekly Live Group Coaching & Training Sessions** with Steve Teneriello and his team.

- **Access to Ready To Launch Campaigns:** Complete with landing pages, sales copy, graphics, and keywords these step-by-step campaign blueprints are available to help you drastically increase lead conversion.

Gain Access to these Bonus Resources, Tools and Training Today by Joining Pay-Per-Click Prosperity.

Get Started and Visit: www.payperclickprosperity.com

Table of Contents

Introduction

PART I: LOST AT SEA

20   **Knowing Your Surroundings:** How To Reach Your
       Very Best Customers, Clients, or Patients Starting Today

37   **When PPC Sharks Attack:** How To Prevent Being
       Eaten Alive By Scammers, Scoundrels, and Fraudsters

PART II: THE 3 SURVIVAL NECESSITIES

60   **Building Shelter:** The 6 Ways To Increase Lead
       Volume That Your PPC Manager Doesn't Want You To
       Know About

75   **Hunting Your Food:** Discover How to Uncover Your
       Prospects' Pain and Turn Them Into New Customers,
       Clients or Patients Following These 10 Killer Ad
       Copy Rules.

103   **Finding Water:** The 5 Landing Page Mistakes Your
       PPC Manager is Making and How to Fix Them

PART III: IT'S GO TIME

122   **Using The First Aid Kit:** 7 Common Google AdWords
       Budget Bleeders and How to Fix Them

135   **Rationing Your Supplies:** A Lesson In Google Math
       They Didn't Teach You In School

151   **From Surviving To Thriving:** 21 Proven AdWords
       Strategies to Outsmart Your Competitors and Get More
       For Less

Conclusion

Introduction

Why Now Is The Time To Start Mastering AdWords, Even If You Haven't Had Success In The Past.

Google AdWords® has changed the marketing game, and it's never going back.

The tremendous possibilities for internet advertising have ushered in a new age. We're all living in a marketing world where the only surefire thing is that you will either *sink or swim*. Huge potential for marketing success is out there through Google AdWords, but very few people know how to make it work. Learning the program takes time, effort, and innovation.

It's possible that you've tried Google AdWords in the past and were *lost at sea*. You may be trapped in a bad relationship with your current pay-per-click manager, wasting money month after month. Now you're struggling just to stay afloat!

Maybe you feel like you're drowning.

But *look up*! This is your chance!

You're holding the *Google AdWords Survival Guide*, which means there's still hope for your company's AdWords yet. I'm throwing you a life preserver, and all you have to do is *grab ahold!* This isn't the time to let your business drown. Now is the time to invest in PPC advertising, even if you haven't had success in the past. Now is the time to thrive.

There has never been more opportunity to seize control of your ad spend and make every penny count towards bringing in calls.

There have never been more tools and technology at your disposal to help you reach your ideal customer and generate high quality leads from targeted ad campaigns.

There has never been more concentrated demand, and it's *still growing* – people are looking for your products and services right now on their desktops, laptops, tablets, and smartphones, all through online search engines as you are reading this.

And you may not believe it when I say this now, but give me time and I'll prove it: *there has never been a brighter future for your own business.*

When you have an intimate knowledge of how to use Google AdWords like I do, you can market on a whole new level of efficiency. You can enhance your control of your advertising spend and update your ads with *immediate visibility and performance.* You can target potential customers by area, keyword, and even their IP address. You can take advantage of rapidly expanding mobile search. You can track your performance metrics precisely and comprehensively to calculate the returns on your investment, and you can grow those returns into consistently sizeable profits.

So what are you going to do? Doggy-paddle around with outdated advertising media and inefficient AdWords management until your arms (and your budget) give out?

Or do you dare to set foot on dry land?

Don't settle for AdWords mediocrity. You can choose to take control and get proven results from Google®. You can completely eliminate wasted Google AdWords marketing spend, outsmart your competitors, and acquire new clients through pay-per-click advertising. *It all starts right here.*

Right now, you may still feel like you can never turn your advertising around and make Google AdWords work for you. You're still adrift in a raging sea. But now you're holding the lifesaver – it's the book that's in your hands.

What To Expect From This Book

Here's What You'll Learn From *The Google Adwords Survival Guide* And How It Will Prepare You For Marketing Success

If you want to outsmart your competitors, put an end to bleeding budgets once and for all, and quickly attract new clients, customers, or patients, this book has the most important information you'll ever read. Why?

Because dozens of companies in your local area, including yours, are competing for pivotal exposure on search engines like Google. Every business wants to acquire new leads on AdWords, and 97% of them are failing to get results. If you become the one business in your market to play the pay-per-click game correctly, you will be *seizing control* of your consumer audience in a way unlike any other medium can achieve.

Google AdWords is the epitome of *sink-or-swim* advertising – you either win or you lose. The odds are stacked against you when you're not staying on top of things. Unfortunately, the chances are high that you're currently set up to fail – and it's not your fault.

That's why you opened this book. You can tell by the way that your ads are managed that you need all the help you can get. It is *obvious* that the company handling your Google AdWords campaigns does not have your best interests at heart. There are simple, no-brainer campaign management practices being completely overlooked and costing you precious advertising dollars.

But there's good news: the majority of your closest competitors are guaranteed to be set up for failure in the same exact way.

How do I know this?

With more than a decade of experience and over one million generated leads under my belt for my clients, it's fair to say I've learned a thing or two about making the phone ring for local businesses. I've seen all types of dangerous AdWords scenarios, and I've helped my clients survive them all. My approach delivers unbeatable Google AdWords success by uniting the technology, skills, and expertise required to convert clicks to leads. I have turned around hundreds of failing campaigns throughout the years, and I can do the same for you.

Too many local businesses feel like they're prey in the Google AdWords wild. My *Survival Guide* is intended to turn that dynamic completely around. I want to outline my winning approach to you and set you up with the tools and know-how you need to make your own account perform at optimal levels.

In this book, you will learn:

- The vocabulary of Google AdWords – knowing how to speak the language is a huge first step!

- How to tell if you're in a bad relationship with your Google AdWords manager, and if they're inhibiting your performance.

- The tools and technologies that make up the foundation of any successful pay-per-click ad campaign.

- The 10 step-by-step rules of writing killer ad copy.

- Why a strategically designed and well-crafted landing page can be the difference between a winning campaign and a losing one.

- How to leverage the features available with Google AdWords – these include ad extensions, keyword tracking, area targeting, and so much more.

- 21 proven strategies for outsmarting your competition.

- Where to find bonus online resources to continue your AdWords training and get even more from your PPC budget this year.

Essentially, the whole point of this book is to help you survive any AdWords scenario. I want to help you get your head above water, reach dry land, set up a stable camp, and take advantage of all the resources you need – not just to survive, but to feel in control again. That's what the *Google AdWords Survival Guide* is really about.

So take a deep breath! Pretty soon, we're going to dive in to your current AdWords account. I'm sure you're already fed up and frustrated with the results you're getting, not to mention all of the wasted dollars that don't deliver a return on your investment. Why continue to put up with it? With just a few adjustments, you could be well on your way towards turning around your campaign performance and making Google your best source of new revenue ever!

Let's talk about survival skills. Here are some of the abilities you'll be taking away from this book and how they will directly increase your returns:

Acquire PPC Leads at a Cost That Makes Sense

Every ounce of your advertising spend will be accounted for when you follow my best practices. You will know exactly how much it should cost you to acquire a new lead, where you are overpaying, and how to trim the fat. As you're reading, you may need to do some on-the-go math, so keep your calculator handy.

I will walk you through the systematic and scalable approach I've built towards getting more opportunities at a predictable cost that *makes sense*. Together, we will implement smart strategies such as timing your ads to capitalize on peak-demand hours, using Google's ad extensions to increase lead conversions, taking advantage of responsive features to target the growing market of mobile searchers, and much, much more. You will never feel like your precious advertising dollars are being wasted again. Finally, there's dry land in sight!

Reduce Your Current Spend & Double Your Performance

With this book, you'll learn how to stop the bleeding on your advertising budget by repairing and improving your relationship with Google.

All too often, local small businesses get trapped in contracts with national Google Resellers who basically steal from them – in my mind, taking money off the top of a company's ad spend is theft, plain and simple. Even if they aren't taking outrageous and non-transparent commissions from your budget, though, chances are they still aren't giving your account the attention that it needs, resulting in unsatisfactory returns and waste. If you're stuck in this scenario, this book will help you identify the problems, bandage up the wounds, and get back on your feet with a new AdWords strategy that emphasizes conversion, transparency, and results.

My clients who have come from reseller companies generally save 40-70% in wasted ad spend per month. That's the sort of saving that I want to create for you and your business – and I know that I can.

Enact Up-To-The-Minute Management Strategies

One of the most critical components of building a Google AdWords account that delivers results is having the dedication to capitalize on every potential opportunity. Part of this means spending some money to make money, a concept I know you're familiar with as a business owner – but what's even more important than the financial investment is the time investment it takes to keep up with the fast-pace changes of the internet.

For a business owner willing to budget the time to properly market their service (or to find a pay-per-click managing company that actually has their back), Google AdWords is the best way to generate leads.

Why?

Because AdWords can be updated in real-time. Not only do you only pay for the advertising space when it is being actively seen (i.e. clicked on), but you can also stop or start your advertising whenever you want and it will *immediately take effect.* Make a change today and have results by dinner time.

Are you ready to take on the best and most dynamic marketing tool in existence? Then you'll need this book at your side. In this *Survival Guide,* you'll find the valuable how-to breakdowns of proven management strategies such as the following:

- **How to outsmart competitors with deep pockets:** Set yourself apart from the rest of the pack. Use Google AdWords in ways that distinguish your business and put you in control of your market.

- **How you can use AdWords to target the different types of customers:** We will break down your customer base into three distinct profiles and discuss how to create ad copy that appeals to each one.

- **My proven daily management formula for driving in high quality leads:** Increase your click-through-rates, conversion, and lead quality with laser-focused keyword strategies that employ more effective research.

- **The combination of tools, technologies, and systems you need to get the most out of Google AdWords:** Pay-per-click optimization, like anything else, requires the right tools. Learn where to start and where to end up with my comprehensive walk-throughs.

"All of this sounds great, Steve," you're probably thinking, "But I've been burned by Google AdWords before…why should I trust you?"

I'm glad you asked.

Three Powerful Reasons to Believe What I Say

1. I have been managing Google AdWords campaigns since Google first introduced the program back in 2002.

2. To date, I have generated more than one million leads for local businesses and have successfully managed campaigns at all levels with budgets ranging from $1,000 to $250,000 per month.

3. Over the last 4 years, I have retained 98% of my client base. Business owners are overwhelmingly satisfied with what my methods get them, and I have a world-class team of rock stars who are committed to client success.

More than anything, I'm proud of that last number. Pretty soon I'm going to give you the dirt on the most popular publicly traded reseller companies, and one of the first issues I'll point out is that they hardly ever take the time to know their own clients. The result is that they have outrageous turnover rates. I know because those unsatisfied customers make up a large portion of my own client base. You might not even know that you're being taken advantage of right now! But soon, you'll be out of the water and in control of your own destiny once again.

I'm also going to show you my management process and how my company leverages tools, technology, technical aptitude, and direct response advertising techniques to make the phone ring consistently for our clients.

So that's what you're about to get from *The Google AdWords Survival Guide*. I'm here for you as an AdWords expert, as your guide, and as your friend. After reading some of what I have to say, you may regret your past AdWords practices. You may regret signing that prior contract that got you where you are right now. But you are never going to regret picking up this book.

Welcome to the *Survival Guide*. Now let's get started.

— Steve Teneriello
Google AdWords Lead Generation and Conversion Specialist

PART I: LOST AT SEA

Understanding the Basics of Google AdWords
and How to Recognize PPC Failure

1

Knowing Your Surroundings

How To Reach Your Very Best Customers, Clients, or Patients Starting Today

1.1 - I'll Be Your Guide

Steve Teneriello: How The Master Of Lead Generation Got To Be Where He Is Today

I don't want to bore anyone with my life's story, but I do think it's important for you to know who I am and where I came from. You may find you have some things in common with me, and it might help you get a better sense of where I'm coming from with some of the against-the-grain advice I'm going to give. Besides – I'm never boring!

So here goes. I am the product of a middle class family. I was lucky enough to grow up with a computer in my family's apartment. It was a Macintosh, and I was the only 4th grader on the block typing up his book reports. I used PrintShop to make greeting cards, and I can't remember how many times I died of dysentery playing *The Oregon Trail*. I used floppy discs and a dot matrix printer that would take hours to print off a finished product – not to mention all of the times it got jammed with those perforated holes in those infuriating plastic feeders.

It was with that first computer that I printed out the flyers for "Steve's Odd Job Services" in the sixth grade. I would advertise to the top old age homes in Malden, Massachusetts, doing just about everything: cleaning floors, taking out trash, putting groceries away, raking leaves, and shoveling out cars in snow storms. I would take my Huffy bike and travel throughout

Malden in response to my elderly clients' needs – making ten bucks at a time for services delivered. I was kicking the paperboy's ass in monthly sales, and was eventually able to leverage the local neighborhood kids to scale my odd job service. Business boomed – there wasn't anyone over seventy years old who didn't know my name.

Point is, I was born an entrepreneur and was lucky enough to have parents who were also entrepreneurial. I grew up in a big Italian family of small business owners. Ever since I was a kid, I have seen first-hand the triumphs and failures that come with owning your own business. From the rush and excitement of bringing on a new account to the stress and struggle in making a payroll, I was exposed to it all, and it was with those experiences in mind that I have followed my passion for helping business owners grow.

Over the last decade, I've generated well over one million inbound leads for hundreds of local business owners. I have taken startups to million dollar companies in less than a year. I've grown quarter million dollar companies to more than four million a year businesses, and I've done it more times than I can count with the power of Google AdWords.

My love for AdWords happened completely by accident. I was originally a band geek and played the trumpet...I still play it to this day. I figured I was destined to become a music teacher. In fact, I consider my music teachers Mr. Kaplan and Mr. Lutz to be two of the most important influences in my life. They instructed me in more than just notes on a page: they taught me powerful life lessons about leadership, the value of competitive spirit, and how to sell.

Yes, sell.

See, every year, my class would have a band trip, and the only way for me to get on the bus and go to New York City or Virginia Beach or Toronto was to go out and sell advertising space to local businesses for our yearly holiday concert guide. Mom and Dad were not footing the bill. Four full page ads would earn me my ticket. Cold calling local businesses and closing deals was a skill I picked up in middle school.

Long story short, the music teacher thing didn't manifest itself. Instead, after leaving UMass, I took a job as a field technician for a national home improvement company. As a young pup, I learned the ins and outs of business from lead generation to contract fulfillment.

After a couple of years, I decided to take my experience on the road. I wanted to start my own home improvement company. At this time, vinyl siding and window replacements were very popular, so I focused there.

Keep in mind, I can't use a hammer to save my life. I found sub-contractors who could do all of the work, and I focused on sales and marketing. I was good at the selling part, but the marketing was a challenge. Competitors, including the company I'd once worked for, were advertising on TV and radio. They could afford yellow page ads and had fruitful direct mail budgets. I was a very small fish in an ocean of sharks. I failed miserably in trying to get new leads. I knocked on doors, printed out flyers, and even saved up enough to drop 5,000 postcards in a city – only to receive one call. It was from a guy who wanted me to take him off of my mailing list.

Things weren't working out, and I was failing fast. I couldn't operate at the same level as my competition, and my grass-roots guerilla marketing was slow and choppy.

It was right when I was at the end of my rope – and right about the time of the internet bubble – that I discovered a brand new lead generation service. It was called Service Magic. Mind you, at the time, barely anyone used the internet. A website was something only very large companies had. But something about the potential of online marketing got my attention.

Service Magic would team you up with people who were searching online for prescreened home improvement professionals – I figured I had nothing to lose, so I joined the program.

At first, I didn't get much activity. I was, I believe, the only small company who bought into this idea of internet advertising. At best, I would average 3-4 leads per month...but this was all I needed. One siding or window job would hold me over for 90 days, and Service Magic could get me that.

Then things changed fast, and there was a huge shift almost overnight in how consumers were using the website. Before you knew it, I was getting about half a dozen leads per week, and I finally had a consistent business. That was all it took for me to realize there was something to this whole "internet marketing" thing.

I built a website using FrontPage and taught myself how to code with HTML. I was one of the first home improvement contractors in my market with a website. I studied how Service Magic got their leads. They were using banner ads and advertising on sites like Yahoo (at the time, Google really did not exist as it does today). I built a second site, one that competed locally against Service Magic. I set up an account with a company called Overture – which is now considered the inventor of pay-per-click advertising. My ads were going directly up against Service Magic. I was pulling in more leads than I could handle, and the home improvement part of my business ultimately started to recede into the background.

Lead generation was what I was all about.

I started to get calls from other contractors who were buying into Service Magic and had noticed my competing website. I had never intended to sell leads, nor did I ever intend to compete directly against Service Magic – my site only had a few pages, and its original goal was to supplement my sales funnel. But there I was, generating more and more interest from other contractors, and finally I found myself in the internet advertising business.

Fast forward a decade and a half later – and here we are.

Let's get right down to brass tacks. There is a reason why you decided to pick up this book.

This book is for you if you are a small business owner looking to grow. You know, just like I did, that internet marketing is the best way to get your business off the ground, but you don't know where to begin.

This is for you if you heard of me through my webinars, through a friend, or through a package at your doorstep – hey, what can I say? I'm a marketing expert, I know how to get your attention.

This book is for you if you're stuck in a bad relationship with the company already managing your Google AdWords campaigns. Perhaps you've lost some confidence since you're not getting the results you expected you would get. Or maybe you have a PPC manager who's running everything and telling you it's all okay, that he's giving you *lots of impressions,* that your

CTR and your CPC, your ABC, your XYZ and your C3P0 are all doing just fine – but you can't help thinking that he's just blowing smoke, since your phone is just not ringing.

This book is for you if you'd like to know just what this whole PPC thing is about so you can get a clearer picture on how to manage it better.

This book is definitely for you if you have gone through multiple PPC managers, have been in one bad relationship after the next, and burned through more budget than you could handle. If you're the guy that looks at AdWords and says, "*Hey – why didn't I buy any Google stock?* I'm the reason they're still in business!" then this book was written with you in mind.

This book is for you if you feel like you're lost at sea. You set off in your vessel – your local business. You thought you had everything you needed for your voyage. How could you have counted on this? Now you're cast adrift in an age of internet marketing that is more than what you bargained for when you climbed aboard. You're stranded in a vast ocean of information, and you're just wishing for dry land – and maybe for people to start using yellow pages again like they used to. But that's not how it works anymore! You're surrounded by harsh, unfamiliar wilderness, and you're going to need to adapt if you want to survive.

But don't worry, because no matter which of these buckets you fit in, I'm throwing you a lifesaver. My name is Steve Teneriello, and I'm here to share with you some of my very best secrets and the time tested strategies you can implement to turn Google AdWords into a money maker for your business – and potentially the most dominant marketing tool in your arsenal.

Depending on how well or how poorly your AdWords account is managed, PPC advertising can be your ace in the hole or a grenade in your trench. Google AdWords is like no other marketing technology to date in that it is incredibly dynamic and operates in *real-time*…we'll get further into what I mean by that later down the line. For now, just know that understanding how to properly manage a Google AdWords account will put you miles ahead of your competition – and by picking up this book, no matter the reason, you've taken the right first step.

Alright, enough about me. Let's talk AdWords.

1.2 Google AdWords 101

First of all, we'll give ourselves a definition of AdWords that we can really work with:

> ✪ **Google AdWords** – A web application offered by the search engine Google that allows companies to advertise their products and services by bidding on the relevant keywords for their local markets. When Google users search for the terms that were bid on, the most successful bidders wind up at the top of the results. Users pay Google their bid amount each time that their ad is clicked, hence it's known as pay-per-click (PPC) advertising.

Remember, this is just the basic definition: we're going to delve a lot further into what makes a bid "successful," what the best "relevant keywords" are, and a whole host of more nuanced examinations. However, this will be our starting point. At its core, Google AdWords is a PPC marketing tool that brings consumers and advertisers together based on what phrases the consumers search and the advertisers pursue.

Google initially released AdWords with cost per click pricing in February of 2002. Now, AdWords is Google's *main source of revenue.* In 2013, Google surpassed $50 billion in annual revenue...and it hasn't slowed down since then! They really have revolutionized the advertising game completely, and quarter over quarter Google AdWords has been one of fastest growing advertising sources for businesses. Like I said, AdWords changed the game...and now it's *anybody's game to win.*

AdWords offers its users all of the following abilities. You can:

- Target and serve ads to consumers in the cities, towns, and counties you work in.
- Control your advertising costs from minute to minute.
- Compete on an equal playing field.
- Turn on, slow down, turn off, and ramp up ads in real-time.
- Track important metrics to help you measure your success.

Originally, Google AdWords was structured so that advertisers would pay a monthly amount, and Google would manage their campaigns for them.

Soon thereafter, they created a "self-service campaign platform" to allow small businesses to manage their own AdWords accounts. In 2004, they launched the Google Advertising Professional (GAP) program to certify AdWords account managers – this later became the Google AdWords Certification program, which has proven to be a pretty mixed bag. I'll walk you through the different types of PPC managers and agencies in the next section. For now, just know that the company that manages your AdWords account has *a lot of responsibility* to your business, and you owe it to yourself to make sure that they have your best interests at heart.

Can you be your own PPC manager? It's certainly possible, but you really need to know what you're doing. Google AdWords offers budget-control in real-time, IP address exclusion, click-tracking, remarketing, and so much more – can you use all of those advertising tools together to their fullest potential and have time to run your business? I've created a comprehensive program that gives you all of the tools, technology, training, and live coaching you need to control your Google AdWords destiny. It's called Pay-Per-Click Prosperity. Visit my website steveten.com for details. We'll talk about this later as well.

In a word, successful Google AdWords management is about optimization. That means taking the monthly budget that you put into AdWords and doing as much as possible with it. You will need to make every penny count by targeting the right customers, using the right technology, writing efficient ad copy, and controlling your budget correctly. There are a lot of "ifs" involved, and when the pieces don't come together, you could have a disaster on your hands.

Fortunately, you've got your *Survival Guide* to help you through it.

1.3 - Why Google?

So, inquiring minds want to know: what makes Google AdWords so special? There are so many different types of marketing, and so many of them seem, on the surface, to be less time-intensive than AdWords – so why even bother?

The reason so many business owners are turning to Google AdWords for their internet marketing is because it is the fastest way to send your message out the door so it can start generating leads. AdWords allows you to get in front of your target customer in a matter of minutes. Additionally, Google is where the lion's share of people now go to start their buying process. It's way faster than direct mail, TV, print media, radio, and all the rest because it's all online, and it's more effective than email because it reaches the broadest consumer audience available. You don't need their email addresses – you just need to know what they're *looking for.*

Even more important is the fact that, with Google AdWords, you can control your costs based on the consumption of your ads! Imagine if you only had to pay for direct mail advertising that you knew was getting noticed. Wouldn't you feel more in control of your marketing right off the bat? With a Google AdWords account, you control just about everything. You can even track how many people are clicking on your PPC ad links, how many of those people are engaging with your site, and how many of those readers are interested enough to call! In some ways, it's a micro-manager's dream come true. It's also capable of delivering the best return on investment (ROI) you could ever hope to get from your advertising, especially as a local business.

I mentioned that Google AdWords reaches the broadest consumer audience out there, and I wasn't kidding. The sheer volume of prospects that AdWords gives you access to is mind boggling. Google is, of course, the most popular search engine in the world, and as such they have a lot of users. How many, you ask? As of the end of 2014, Google search boasted the following:

The Statistics of Search[1]

- Over 40,000 searches every second.
- 3.5 billion searches every day.
- 1.2 trillion searches every year.
- More than 65% share of the global search market.

When you use Google AdWords, you're communicating with a consumer base like no other in history. Google is the undisputed King of Search, and every successful attempt to capitalize on that phenomenal market starts with an in-depth knowledge of what AdWords is and how it works.

And as Google AdWords progresses, so does its targeting. I would imagine that in the next few years you'll be able to target consumers by age, income, and other demographic and affinity information.

It's more than just volume that makes the Google search market so desirable: it's also that fact that Google itself is such an adaptable and intuitive program. Anyone can use Google. All you need to do is type what you want and press ENTER. And now, anyone can use Google from any device. Smartphone and tablet usage is on the rise, and Google makes it easy to take your devices with you straight to the source of the problem.

In the store and need to make a quick price comparison? Now you can Google the answer you need right in the television department at Best Buy.

Need to know where the nearest gas station is relative to your current location? Google it on your iPhone, and there will even be a clickable address that brings you a map of how to get there.

Want to know when the next time you can see *The Avengers* in your town is? Google the title on your tablet or Kindle Fire and you'll be taken to a list of show times at a cinema near you. Not into the whole 3-D thing? Neither am I – so if I google *The Avengers* and only 3-D shows come up at the first local theater, I just flip to the next one.

And that's not even all, because the best part is yet to come: Google gives advertisers the ability to track consumers in ways never before thought possible. PPC advertising gets more sophisticated almost every day. You can now view your demographics with regards to when they search for your products, how they reach your website, and why they call you for help. You can even tell what landing page of yours resulted in them giving you a call! It's seriously scary how well you can get to know your customers through a properly optimized Google AdWords account. Here are some more abilities you'll have for prospect tracking, just to name a few:

- See how many people saw your ads and decided to click.
- Record rates of conversion for independent landing pages.

- Track specific site ad clickers by their IP addresses with the right tracking technology.

- Design your strategy based on the most-searched keywords.

- See where your customers come from to get to your site.

- Follow your customers with ads after they leave.

That's online marketing power, baby. Google AdWords can be the greatest investment you'll ever make as a business owner. You just need to know how to keep up with Google's world.

1.4 - The Future of Online Advertising

Right about now, you may be wondering, "What the heck happened? Just a few years ago it was good enough to have a prominent ad in the Yellow Pages and a decent website – now I need to *track my customers' IP Addresses?* When did marketing get to be like this?"

Honestly, I'm with you 100%. The new world of marketing and advertising is brutally fast-paced and complicated. It feels even faster after you've gotten to know Google for a while. In just the last year, Google has released about a dozen updates and enhancements to Google AdWords. As a PPC consultant, I've had to monitor and preempt those changes for all of my clients. It can be exhausting.

But at the end of the day, we marketers do this because it's what the people want. The driving force behind all of this change is the recent shift in consumer buying behavior. The emphasis on physical presence is gone, and now it's all about your ability to go digital, to be readily available in their pocket, and to schedule service at the touch of a button.

And can you blame them? The Internet Age has made researching and purchasing products a dramatically simpler and more convenient process.

Who needs CDs when you can have all of the songs you want in your iTunes library?

Who needs yellow pages when you can type in exactly what you want and have the search engine bring the phone numbers to you?

Who needs a Blockbuster or a Borders when you can buy movies and books on the go to watch and read wherever you please?

Now we're starting to ask ourselves whether or not the other mediums that we've come to know, love, and even rely on as advertisers will even be in existence anymore going forward. For instance, now that Netflix allows you to stream TV on your computer whenever you want and they're coming out with their own wildly popular shows that can be watched by the season, one has to wonder if cable TV is even going to last for the next decade. Same goes for the radio: now that Sirius FM allows people to listen to precisely the type of music they want, will basic radio stations even be necessary going forward?

And what will be the next social media boom? What will be the next Facebook and send everyone reeling with a new and better way to harvest demographic data? Or the next YouTube that introduces a completely new method of targeted video advertising? Pinterest, Buzzfeed, and even more modern sites have become central hubs for marketers to reach specific audiences with picture and video advertisements that function differently than ever before.

Google is definitely the leader, but it's not the only player with a hat in the ring. Advertising in general has grown to be a totally different game. And who knows how it will grow from here? I can't see into the future, but I've seen the present reality of online advertising up close and personal. I know PPC marketing like the back of my hand, and I know exactly what the search market is capable of. That's enough that I can always stay one step ahead.

Get Your Frame Of Reference With The Google AdWords Lexicon

Before we go any further, I have to warn you: there's some seriously technical talk up ahead.

Luckily, I'm not a huge fan of jargon myself, and I only use the technical terms when it's necessary. Still, I thought it might be helpful to include a glossary of common vocabulary terms that are important for understanding PPC as we move ahead. We'll start with the "success metrics," by which I mean the numbers that help you measure your AdWords performance.

You need to be able to identify these terms while you're lost at sea:

- **Impressions** – User views. Your ads come up when people search the keywords you bid on – your impression count is the number of times that your ads are actually seen. Although having many impressions means your ads are visible, a high impression rate without clicks spells trouble. As a success metric, impression counts are just a piece of the puzzle. Having a ton of impressions with little traffic to show for it is a cause for concern.

- **Clicks** – The actions that follow your ad copy link in the search results to your dedicated landing page – this causes Google to charge you your bid amount. When I talk about "clicks" as a success metric, I'm talking about the number of times your ads are clicked on, not the clicks it takes to get to the ad copy. A valid click requires that a person searches for the keyword you've bid on, sees your ad in their results, and decides to follow the link with the intent of learning more.

- **CTR (Click-Through Rate)** – This is the number of impressions your ads receive divided by their number of clicks. What results from that equation is the percentage of times your ads are seen that result in clicks. CTR is a valuable indicator of ad optimization and how well consumers are responding to your sales copy. A healthy campaign will traditionally have a high and healthy click-through rate.

- **CPC (Cost Per Click)** – This term refers to how much you pay Google each time your ad is clicked. You can improve your cost per click by improving the Quality Score of your campaign setup and by optimizing your ad copy. We'll talk about Quality Score in a bit.

- **Conversion** – The rate at which clicks on your ads become leads in your sales funnel. Your conversion rate is undeniably the most important success metric of all.

Now we'll transition from defining success metrics to learning the core components of a Google AdWords campaign:

- ✪ **Ad Campaign** – A focused pay-per-click effort on a single product or service. An ad campaign should include a direct offer, (i.e. a form of consumer incentive). Built into each ad campaign is an assemblage of the following:

    - ✪ **Adgroups** – Subsets of an AdWords campaign. Each contains its own set of relevant keywords. Typically, a campaign will have several separate ad groups categorized by similar services or search terms.

    - ✪ **Ads** – The individual components of each adgroup containing the sales copy visible to a consumer in their search results.

    - ✪ **Keywords** – Search terms that are directly relevant to your marketing strategy. When a user inputs these words or phrases into a Google search, you want your company's offers to appear among the ads that result.

    - ✪ **Ad Extensions** – Features of an ad that show extra information, such as clickable phone numbers, searchable addresses, or DOWNLOAD buttons.

    - ✪ **Bids** – The amount of money you establish as a maximum for how much you are willing to pay for a click. This number, in conjunction with your campaign's Quality Score, determines your positioning. Bidding more (generally) makes your ads more visible. Most small businesses tend to manage their bids automatically – but that doesn't mean you can simply not pay attention to your cost per click!

- ✪ **Targeting** – The process of selecting specific geographic locations to market to via PPC ads. Yet another feature of AdWords.

- ✪ **Budget** – The maximum amount of your AdWords spend, which can be customized daily. Each click that you receive on your PPC ads takes its cost from your budget. When you reach your daily budget limit, your ads stop appearing.

- **Google Quality Score** – The metric Google uses on a 1-10 scale to determine the overall quality of your ads and landing pages triggered by a specific keyword. The higher the Quality Score, the more relevant and useful your ad is to someone searching with a specific keyword. You have to keep in mind that, as a search engine, Google actually has two customers: its advertisers and the people who use it for search. Their first and foremost priority is their searcher satisfaction – advertisers come decidedly second. The Quality Score makes sure you are keeping the results clean and relevant to Google's search customers.

  Here's an example of what I mean. It seems like there is at least one major news story or celebrity scandal per month. Something like this will almost always guarantee a ton of internet traffic. So a savvy advertiser, back before Quality Score existed, would bid on terms involving the news story or celebrity scandal to capture traffic and serve their ad. Let's say the ad was for pimple cream. Celebrity scandal X has absolutely nothing to do with pimple cream Y, but the advertiser would make them appear for the same keywords. However, due to Google's stricter standards for relevancy, this ad would most likely receive a low Quality Score if it were created today, and as a result it would not serve or would only serve for a very short period of time.

  When the descriptions of your product or service are vague and seem to apply to a broad and nebulous search audience – or to no particular audience at all – you risk losing ground on your Quality Score. This can seriously cost you in the long run, so we'll be sure to go over some methods of improving and maintaining Quality Score across your campaigns.

- **Landing Page** – The web page that your PPC ads direct traffic to. This should be optimized for maximum lead conversion – which we will get into!

We'll have more opportunities to learn the important definitions of Google AdWords terms as the book continues, so I'll leave some to be discussed in more relevant contexts. Of all the vocabulary we'll learn, though, no definition is more important than the following:

✪ **Conversion-Based Approach** – A strategy of pay-per-click account management that bases its entire philosophy on how effectively your ad campaigns are able to convert clicks into leads and return on investment. The primary reason you want to learn how to develop the right mix of bid management, budget control, and ad copy for PPC marketing is to make the phone ring. As you read this book, you are going to find I am 100% conversion minded. It's all about leads and sales in my book. It's really the most important metric for a small business leveraging Google AdWords.

The conversion-based approach is what our primary concern as Google AdWords survivors is going to be. We'll make your business get by and eventually thrive with strategies that put lead volume and lead quality first so that you can see the value of PPC.

How Search Works

The results-generating formula for a search engine as large and influential as Google would obviously be immensely complicated. But you don't need to know any of that! All you need to understand are the basic stages of how the pay-per-click process happens:

1. **Real-Time Auction** – All bidding for keywords is performed in real-time, which means competition between companies in the same market can be fierce. Bids can be adjusted, paused, and restarted at any time, meaning that bidding in the most efficient way possible takes vigilance!

2. **Keyword Strategy** – This is the list of search terms that you want to rank for with your PPC ads. If you own a pizzeria in Hoboken, New Jersey, for instance, you'd want your ads to show up when a person types in "pizza delivery Hoboken." But depending on your market and the demographic you're advertising to, keyword strategies can vary wildly between local markets.

3. **Ad Placement** – When a Google user searches for a keyword that you bid on, your ad should show up. But where, exactly? The positioning of your ad can depend on your strategy as well

as how you're handling your competition.

4. **Ad** – The ad copy itself is absolutely critical. What phrases grab people's attention? What deals make buyers want to buy?

5. **Click** – When your ad copy is successful and the positioning is right, the ad gets clicked. But you need to make sure those clicks are resulting in leads being created! In the same way that impressions are only valuable if they're generating clicks, clicks are only really valuable if they are converting into leads at a decent rate.

6. **Landing Page** – This is where the people who click on your ads wind up, and it ought to contain enough enticing material and strategic assets that it makes clickers transition into actual leads.

7. **Lead Generation** – How well are your ad campaigns bringing in potential buyers? How visible are you, and how truly effective is your ad copy? The central purpose of every ad campaign you create is to design a sales funnel that brings in high quality leads consistently and at a *cost that makes business sense.*

The point of this book is to optimize every stage of your pay-per-click management. That means being willing to outpace your competition by investing the time and money necessary into Google AdWords to generate impressive ROI. It means researching and creating the most potent keyword strategies possible. It means acquiring the positioning that your ad campaigns need through balanced dedication. It means learning how to write ad copy that practically forces your ideal customer to pick up the phone and call you. It means getting the most possible clicks at the lowest possible cost. It means investing time in landing pages that convert, and making sure they always do their job.

And finally, it means getting *real results* and knowing that for every dollar you invest in Google AdWords you can expect a healthy and fruitful return.

There is so much to learn about Google AdWords and so many challenges involved in making PPC advertising consistently work. But I know it's possible because I've done it, and so can you. All it takes is having a strong will to survive.

BONUS RESOURCES FOR "KNOWING YOUR SURROUNDINGS"

Get Steve's AdWords Survival Cheat Sheet ($49 value):

This one pager will be your best friend when you are attempting to navigate the choppy waters of Google AdWords. It includes:

1. Google AdWords Vocabulary You Need to Know.

2. The Anatomy of a Winning Google AdWords Campaign.

3. The Basic Survival Rules for Making Google AdWords work.

**Join Pay-Per-Click Prosperity – the place for better Google AdWords performance – and access this resource today.
Go to: payperclickprosperity.com**

CHAPTER 1 SURVIVOR'S SUMMARY

This chapter introduced your guide, Steve Teneriello, and his background before becoming a lead generation and conversion specialist. It also provided the basic definitions of PPC: the "Google AdWords Lexicon" identified the most important success metrics and campaign components. Finally, we discussed why Google AdWords is the future of advertising.

Your takeaways from this chapter should be what PPC is, how search works, and why Google AdWords has changed marketing.

Test Your Survival Skills: *(Find answers on page 190)*

1. To determine your click-through rate (CTR), divide the number of _____ your ad received by the number of times it was clicked.

2. Worldwide, people use Google to make _____ searches every day and _____ every second.

3. All bidding for keywords in AdWords is performed in _____, which means they can be adjusted, paused, and restarted whenever you want.

2 | When PPC Sharks Attack

How To Prevent Being Eaten Alive By Scammers, Scoundrels, and Fraudsters

2.1 - A Tale of Two Google AdWords Advertisers

It was the best of times, it was the worst of times. It was the age of optimized marketing spend, it was the epoch of unsatisfactory ROI. That's because thousands of American business owners have started investing in Google AdWords to promote their businesses in the past few years, and it has not worked out for everyone! When used properly, Google AdWords is a revolution in advertising: it's a dynamic application that allows you to monitor and adjust your ad spend for PPC on the most used search engine ever according to all of the most relevant information in your industry. But the fact of the matter is that there is a right way to manage AdWords – and then there is a very wrong way.

Too many small businesses are doing AdWords the wrong way. They're letting Google resellers and negligent marketing companies take advantage of them, which is why their relationship with Google is costing them money that isn't buying them calls – making Google out to be the bad guy.

And you *may have been one of them.*

It also doesn't help that the rules of the game seem to be constantly changing. The national averages of click costs are rising in just about every industry, and that's no coincidence: between 2012 and 2014, Google made over 70 updates to their algorithm,[2] and at the same time we saw a 26%

increase on what businesses paid for each click.[3]

Plus, the rise of mobile technology has changed the game even more. Nearly 60% of adults now own smartphones,[4] and the number of searches made on devices besides computers is increasing month over month – what's more is that Google's own surveys have found that consumers who searched on mobile were *more likely* to call the business by a margin of 39%.[5] All of this means that your ads had better be responsive to smartphone and tablet usage, which is just another consideration in a host of modern nuances the new age of search has created.

Overall, the AdWords market is more competitive, complicated, and absolutely critical for small businesses to be involved in than ever before, and if you want to be successful, you need to play Google's game on your terms – not someone else's!

So I want to tell you a story. It's an epic of conquest and despair, of seized and lost opportunities, of thrilling adventure and forbidden romance – it's *The Tale of Two Google AdWords Advertisers*. One of these advertisers had success with AdWords through smart strategies. The other did business with a Google reseller and, as a result, couldn't establish enough momentum to get his ad campaigns off the ground. In other words, one swam, and the other sank.

In this chapter, I'm going to pick apart exactly what those two advertisers did and explain why Google operates the way it does. We'll see the two Google AdWords users in action and on their way to their respective ends. At the end of this chapter, I'll provide you with tools and resources you can use to help better understand how to make AdWords work for you.

Like any game, Google AdWords has winners and losers…and the fact that you are reading this means you are half-way down your path to the winner's circle. But which one were you this past year? Let's find out! We'll start with the AdWords advertiser whose account was mismanaged to see how he was taken advantage of, and then we'll talk about the steps to take in order to avoid getting trapped in this type of one-sided relationship. The first thing we'll learn is that the mismanagement wasn't really his fault: his only misstep was signing on to a PPC marketing company that didn't have his best interests at heart.

2.2 - The Sinkers

Regardless of whether or not you had a reseller managing your business's AdWords account, you can pretty easily tell if your AdWords was managed incorrectly. These are the signs:

- You had a huge monthly bill but no visible performance.

- You were in a committed relationship where you had a mandatory minimum budget upfront and had to pay prior to seeing any revenue resulting from the clicks.

- Your bids were too high or too low, and they weren't bringing in the right amount of calls.

- Your site wasn't getting any traffic, and the clicks you did get weren't generating any leads.

- Your ads contained inaccurate information about your company.

- You never actually saw your ads come up online.

Do these warning signs of a failing AdWords account sound familiar to you? Don't feel bad, the current Google AdWords game has far more sinkers than swimmers. That's because, in the open water of Google AdWords management, too many small businesses trust their accounts to PPC sharks. I'm talking about Google resellers.

What is a Google AdWords Reseller?

Let's start by going over exactly what a Google reseller is and what they do. You may know resellers as "Premier Google SMB Partners" – but regardless of what title they use, they have no vested interest in your company, and working with them can only end in pain. Here's why:

In 2007, Google announced that it was going to create a list of certified AdWords resellers to manage their latest advertising application – it was called the Authorized Reseller Program. When it became clear in 2010 that resellers were blatantly taking advantage of the small and medium businesses they sold to, Google abruptly shut the program down.[6] Upon receiving pressure and complaints from the large reseller companies, Google reopened a revision later that year. They claimed the new policy would emphasize increased transparency in reseller behaviors – however, the reality was that Google's only real promise in the legal text was that they would expect resellers to supply some performance metrics, i.e. impressions and click-through rates, as opposed to having no requirements at all. Todd Rowe, Director of Global SMB Sales at Google, clarified after the release that resellers would *not* be obligated to reveal their mark-up rates to advertisers in the revised program.[7]

Resellers are companies who signed up to sell Google AdWords to small businesses like yours in exchange for Google rebates. A large percentage of their employees are typically in sales teams and are not necessarily qualified to advise as PPC specialists.

Frequently, when these resellers manage your account, they charge a preposterous mark-up on clicks that you might not even notice if you weren't familiar with what a direct-billing relationship with Google should look like. In my own experience, I have found clients trapped in these relationships where they were paying 40-70% *more for clicks* than the clicks would have costed on their own. They were not in control. This number is based on the data I've collected through helping business owners escape the resellers' jaws over the years, but the resellers themselves have never had to comment – for as long as I've been in operation, they have not been required to release their mark-up rates to their customers. In the original program, outright markup on clicks was commonly up to 60%.[8] That's just what the reseller would be taking straight out of your ad spend – those expenses don't even account for other inefficiencies in your budget! The revised program claims to be better, but the numbers tell a very different story. If anything, Google's restrictions have only made resellers trickier and better at manipulating small businesses to get their way.

Basically, Google AdWords changed the entire marketing scene. Now that you can bid on premier advertising positioning in real-time, your internet marketing requires full-time surveillance. The metrics are simple enough – however, tracking these metrics properly involves time, technology, and expertise that most people just don't have or understand. You run a small business, and you need to focus on your customers, clients or patients. The space in your schedule to make constant budget and timing adjustments to your AdWords is understandably limited.

In other words, Google has made it extremely difficult for the average layman to launch and manage his own campaigns. That's why, when these "official" companies approach you, you're happy to sign a contract...even if it doesn't actually guarantee tangible results.

The 5 Lies Google Resellers Will Tell You

Here's how to see through the bad relationships that bleed your budget.

As I mentioned, resellers are generally large companies with large sales teams. The list of authorized resellers mainly consists of national marketing companies and failing local search providers who need to quickly supplement their revenue stream. That's why they signed up to market Google's product to you: they aren't interested in your business or the product, they're just sharks looking to sink their teeth into you.

Once a reseller has sold you an advertising package, they establish a contract (generally a year or less) during which they say they will manage your pay-per-click bids and keyword strategies. You agreed because you figured that, since they were Google-authorized, they were telling you the truth. But the truth was probably the only thing they didn't tell you.

These may sound familiar:

1. **"You're paying for site clicks."** – That's that whole concept of PPC, isn't it? Buying ad clicks through search engine marketing? Well, not when you do it with some of Google's resellers. It is common for a number of Google resellers to ask you for a large sum of money upfront, place some of it in AdWords bids, and keep the rest for themselves. They're able to get away with this by using deceptive software to mask the real market numbers so you never know just how much you're overpaying. The numbers they show you will include large cost margins to throw off the CPC entirely.

2. **"This contract ensures site traffic."** – Your contract likely did not specify how much website traffic you'd receive at all. Rather, it was based on how many impressions you'd get. Impressions are a valuable metric – but they are NOT the same as clicks or calls! Having a keyword impression means your ad shows up when that keyword is searched, but you could have 1000

impressions for keywords that are not relevant to revenue production, and you'd never see a dime of returns. This is just one of the ways that reseller companies get around Google's new rules: by reporting large impression rates for weak keywords, they skew the big picture of your company's web presence.

3. **"Our company is a Google partner."** – Many reseller companies will tell you that they have an "in" with Google. The reality is that Google doesn't really have "partners." All resellers do is sell Google's product for them – Google doesn't take any responsibility or active role in their performance, and they certainly don't let resellers directly influence the order of their search results. They have to compete for positioning with bids just like everybody else.

4. **"We're the PPC experts."** – Companies that apply to be Google resellers do not specialize in PPC – they are sales experts. By virtue of Google's agreement with them, they are required to have a national sales team, but not required to have demonstrable AdWords experience or success. The salesperson you spoke to leading up to the contract signing is not the same person who manages your account, and as soon as you put pen to paper he takes off to make the next sale.

5. **"Our team provides hands-on support."** – Generally, the Google AdWords resellers that people find through searches are international companies. When you've got over 20,000 clients in the U.S., Great Britain, Canada, and Australia, it's tough to keep an eye on all of them! An AdWords account requires constant maintenance for proper optimization, and having one employee running hundreds of accounts at once just isn't going to work. What's even more likely is that your entire account is being run by flashy software that offers no transparency into what you're really paying. Market conditions, bids, and competitive situations are susceptible to change in the blink of an eye, so unless you have an expert monitoring the *minutes and seconds* of your own AdWords campaigns, you're liable to miss out on a huge percentage of what your budget is capable of bringing to the table. Each of my clients has a dedicated

manager and access to an entire team. We use ClickOptix®, a technology solution we built to give clients 100% transparency into critical performance metrics. That's the only *legitimate* way to do business when it comes to running PPC.

You might also be familiar with the result of the Google reseller scam: you watch thousands of dollars slip away from you month after month. Your ads aren't visible when it matters most. The clicks aren't coming in, and when they are they're costing far more than they're worth. Each time you call looking for your account manager, you're connected to a different representative, and you need to explain your business all over again. There's no communication, no transparency, and no results.

Why doesn't Google police their reseller program better? Why do they just let these high-pressure sales organizations mislead and abuse small businesses in their name?

In other words, how do resellers get away with it?

The short answer is that Google does not heavily police this program, nor should they have to. Just like you, they are in business to make money, and if they are able to acquire a new client through a third party, they aren't obligated to worry about how it's done. It's up to you, the AdWords consumer, to do your due diligence and be informed about all of the different options for PPC management that are out there in the marketplace.

Google has given strong consideration to dropping the AdWords resellers program entirely. Back in 2010, before they revamped the ARP, they were starting to see advertiser frustration – and that hasn't gone away. Just recently, Google introduced a new third party policy to make additional changes requiring their resellers to deliver more disclosures to advertisers.[9] Particularly notable is the requirement to list "management fees" on invoices, which was previously not regulated whatsoever. We'll see how these alterations impact the market in 2015.

But I'm not getting my hopes up. Over and over again, these changes have accomplished very little for small businesses. They don't actually force resellers to have more transparency – just more fine print! Google makes millions from AdWords bids whether they are successful or not, and Resellers continue to abuse small businesses by taking huge margins off of their budgets completely unchecked.

Meanwhile, Google rather explicitly states that it takes no responsibility for or part in the reselling process. In their AdWords Reseller Agreement as well as in their Terms and Conditions, Google disassociates itself from the independent sales companies that do their marketing for them. Read it for yourself:

"Resellers shall indemnify and defend Google...for any claims, losses, damages, liabilities, fees, costs, legal fees...and/or expenses incurred by Google as a result of or in relation to any acts or omissions." [10]

What this language means is that Google washes its hands of the whole reseller business altogether. There's no actual connection between the service that Google provides as a search engine and the promises you hear from resellers – call it a lack of accountability if you like, but Google is fairly straightforward in their contracts about the fact that they do not accept responsibility for losses incurred through poor AdWords management. No company is allowed to purchase search result positioning directly, authorized reseller or not.

But it's more than likely that you weren't even aware of this disconnect. That's because resellers are able to conceal the reality of their relationship with Google behind a smoke screen of legal language, buzzwords, and half-truth promises. You know why your contract with them is only 6 months to a year long? Because their priority isn't in keeping clients, it's in selling the product and receiving the rebates from Google in addition to the giant margin they subtract from your ad spend.

It's a numbers game, and in their game you are replaceable. Think about it for a moment: to make your company successful, resellers would need to invest in an increased head count to service and support their accounts. But, as we'll see in the examples ahead, that isn't happening. Why would it when resellers can simply redistribute the work to their existing employees, let the contracts go sour, and then turn around to make more sales? Sales people work on commissions. Talent costs money. Remember, in order to be a Google reseller, you need to have a sales team – that's the most hard-fast requirement the program has! When you really look at it, the reseller business model doesn't factor in your success as an incentive at all.

Examples of Reseller Fraud

Listen, I'm not just blowing smoke: reseller programs have actually told all of the lies that I've mentioned, and I've done the research to prove it.

Every year, tens of thousands of American business owners fall victim to the reseller scam – and many of them still don't even know it. Have you ever done business with one of the following companies? Or have you noticed these business practices in your current PPC relationship? Or are you paying for ads that you can't find when you do a Google Search for them? Then you may be one of the unfortunate small to medium business owners whose AdWords account was mismanaged, resulting in hundreds, even thousands, of budget dollars wasted.

ReachLocal – In their mission statement, this publicly traded company claims that their priority is to "help local businesses all over the world reach more local consumers online." Their company reported revenue of over $514 million in 2013,[11] yet despite the fact that this number had grown over 35% for the year, their employee-to-client ratio has stayed low due to their startling rate of employee turnover. According to ReachLocal's own earning's release in that year, each ReachLocal representative would have to have produced over $540K in annual sales volume – that's assuming equal production for all employees, which is impossible.[12] Profit margins that large with relatively little company expansion should raise some red flags.

When The Wall Street Journal interviewed some of ReachLocal's former executives, they found that most clients' accounts are run by software algorithms. They claim to have more than 24,000 small to mid-sized business clients worldwide, but they have less than 1,000 point-of-contact sales employees. According to the former ReachLocal employees that WSJ interviewed, the salespeople at ReachLocal are not properly trained to troubleshoot or optimize results, although the former ReachLocal President Josh Claman stated their sales team has been "restructured" to address client complaints.[13]

Unsurprisingly, Google declined to comment.

Although ReachLocal claims to be a valuable resource for small business owners, small business customers say otherwise. Since 2009, over

60 complaints have been filed with The Federal Trade Commission regarding ReachLocal's services. One small business owner by the name of Dave Bennet told the story of his increasingly typical interaction with ReachLocal: he signed on for a 4 month contract wherein he would pay $900 a month for the company to create listings in online directories and advertise his service on Google.

In 2009, the annual churn rate of ReachLocal & other publicly traded resellers was 60%. To give you some perspective: churn rates for cell phone and cable providers rarely exceed a few points per quarter.[14]

(**NOTE**: Beware the less-than-one-year contract! This is a tactic employed by AdWords managers whose primary concern is to sell, not to keep! It also is a way to skew retention numbers when it's time to file annual reports.)

When he noticed that calls weren't coming in, he checked the content – only to find that it was entirely inaccurate. ReachLocal had posted the wrong contact information! Even after he called, the problem went unaddressed, so he dropped the service. He'd paid a total of $1,800 for a grand total of 0 calls.

But Dave Bennet is far from being the only case where this happened. In fact, earlier in 2014, WSJ conducted a separate study of ReachLocal's interactions with SMBs and found that small business web ads were frequently not reaching their targets. This article, released in April, included the account of Meghan Goicouria, a business owner in Miami, FL who cancelled her package with ReachLocal after she noticed she was receiving out-of-state calls from Texas and Virginia. In response to her story and similar testimonies, a digital marketing consultant from Australia named Ferdous Haider did some research and found many irrelevant search terms leading to ReachLocal sponsored ads, including several for a Chicago tailoring business that were appearing for New York, Houston, and Los Angeles searches.[15]

ReachLocal is an "SMB" company, which should mean that they specialize in serving small and mid-size businesses, but it's pretty clear that larger companies get preferential treatment. Time and again, ReachLocal's methods have proven inefficient for the local market. Just take it from Forbes, who had this to say about the ReachLocal strategy:

"While companies like ReachLocal try to make this process [of local search marketing] less complicated and offer to do the work on behalf of the advertiser, the junior support staff assigned to these accounts... make it less effective by adding their overhead and markup." [16]

ReachLocal does not have the commitments that they claim to have. There is an alternative agenda here that's fairly plain to see. They don't care about optimizing your ads since that part is all automated – they just care about making the sales, receiving rebates from Google, and taking their margin from your spend. That's why small business owners who work with them are getting chewed up and spit out. What I mean is that their undisclosed retention rates are starting to raise serious concern.

Once again, ReachLocal manages to escape heavy scrutiny by never disclosing their churn rate (that's the rate at which customers cancel their service) – however, market experts' speculations on the number are astronomical. In 2011 (that's *post*-ARP revision), analysts still estimated the churn rate to be between 50% and 70%.[17] Mark-ups were still approximated at 30 to 60%[18] at the time, so it's really no wonder. Still, having half of your on-boarding clients leave is enough to stir up trouble for any industry.

Now we've reached a point in the ReachLocal saga, here in 2014, where the complaints are being heard – and some of the results are not pretty. As I'm writing this book, ReachLocal just posted 3rd quarter losses of $11.3 million for 2014.[19] Their shares are closing at $4.38, when a year ago they were trading at $12.01 – and now their tune is starting to change. In May of this year, ReachLocal CEO Sharon Rowlands wrote a guest article for Forbes decrying the "unsustainable and unacceptable" churn rate of digital marketing to local businesses, which she estimates between 50 and 90%.[20]

I don't know about her, but my digital marketing company has retained 98% of our client base for the last 4 years – and we *only* serve local businesses! This seems like ReachLocal has a *personal problem* to me.

Yodle – Marcos Quinones, a psychotherapist from New York, received a cold call one day from a salesperson who guaranteed that he could get him more clients. Since Quinones was looking to expand, he agreed, and the next thing that he knew he was a Yodle client paying over $2,000 for 3 months of AdWords management service. But that's fine, because you need to spend money to make it, right?

And he did get more calls – the only problem was that they weren't from clients. They were from people who had no idea you needed to pay for psychotherapy. Apparently, Yodle had communicated Quinones' ads so poorly that people thought he was providing a complimentary service. His actual customer base wasn't even seeing the ads! [13]

This is what happens when you have your business represented by an international company with an annual income of $163 million, an international presence, and just over 1000 employees. [21] There's a way that they get to that size, and it isn't by learning about their customers specialties – it's by making the sales. Quinones has said that he received zero customers out of the deal. How can a business expect to generate quality leads from PPC if their ads are this inaccurate?

Yodle is an "All-in-One internet Marketing & Advertising" company with over 40,000 clients, all of them small businesses. Between 2006 and 2011, they experienced a revenue growth of 8,269%, earning them the 21st spot on Deloitte's Fast 500 Ranking. [22] In July of 2014, they filed a form S-1 as one of the first steps towards becoming an IPO. All of this is very impressive! But there's one number that Yodle probably doesn't want you to know about:

Since 2009, the Federal Trade Commission has received more than 180 complaints about Yodle's business practices, and more than 100 of those were filed since 2012. [13]

There's another number that Yodle would rather not disclose: its churn rate. The CEO of the company, Court Cunningham, has said that after a customer stays with Yodle for half a year, the drop-out rate is relatively low (roughly 12% a year). [23] But the reality is that Yodle *only offers* 3 month contracts! Again, the less-than-a-year contract is a common tactic for resellers to distort their projected churn rates: when asked directly about the churn rate estimates of 40 to 50%, the CEO declined to comment.[24]

Cunningham maintains that their churn rate is relatively low for their industry – but let's investigate that statement. What exactly is "relative" to the reseller industry? In 2009, just a few months before Google's revisions to the reseller program, Borrell Associates released an investigative report that showed up to 50% of SMBs who work with resellers quit by 90 days in and up to 90% quit within 6 months.[25] Post-revisions, did the number change? It's unclear. However, confidence is low. At the start of this year, sources were still estimating about a 6.5%-7%[26] monthly churn, which arrives (conservatively) at a 78% annual rate. People like Quinones leave Yodle because the system doesn't work. They find themselves lost in a mess of automation, spending far more than what they receive.

But why do people stay?

Unfortunately, it's because Yodle's salespeople are able to convince customers that paying thousands of dollars every month for some low quality leads is normal for small businesses, and that they just need to raise their internet marketing budgets. Plus, they sink their hooks into small businesses in other ways, including domain ownership and contract termination fees.

Increasingly, it's becoming clear that the satisfaction isn't there: about 75% of SMBs have claimed they would prefer to work with a single digital marketing company, but more than half are working with 2 or more.[27] That means more contracts and more spending with rarely any comparable results.

Moreover, that same study from Thrive Analytics found that nearly 50% of SMBs say their biggest challenge in digital marketing is not having the knowledge they need. Why are people paying for a service they don't understand?

Probably because it seems like it's the only available option. Moving forward, the purpose of this book will be to show you that it isn't.

The reality is that throwing money at the AdWords problem doesn't actually solve it. What small businesses really need is focused account management, which they can't get when their search engine ads are controlled by automations.

Local Search Phone Book Publishers – There's a lot of buzz out there about how local search providers have "succumbed to Google" by becoming resellers, and the rumors are true. Google AdWords is truly the most powerful new advertising medium, and other companies either need to play along or fall behind. This means that the companies offering antiquated options for local search, i.e. phone book listings, are frantically looking for new ways to stay afloat. The two prime examples of this trend are Dex One and SuperMedia, two advertising agencies that recently merged to form Dex Media.

As of April of 2013, Dex One and SuperMedia had combined their money-losing companies into a single corporation, a move they accomplished through declaring a merger bankruptcy.[28] SuperMedia was a Premium Partner from 2012,[29] and Dex Media essentially inherited the status. Now they have over 200,000 advertisers working for them and just over 3,000 employees (again, notice the ratio).[30] But Dex has recently come under attack from ex-clients for failing to provide metrics, honor cancellations, or grant transparency in billing. Moreover, their product is outdated, and the competitors of Dex Media (i.e. daily newspapers) are surging forward to take their marketing share.

Another U.S., phone book publisher turned reseller is the Yellow Pages. Several business owners have reported that Yellow Pages gave them faulty information regarding their relationship with Google, specifically that they've claimed to have priority ranking as a local search engine and can help you get to the top by negotiating with Google from a partner standpoint.[31] This is not true, and it's where the relationship between "partner" and reseller gets blurred. It's important to remember that Google does not allow any company, no matter their budget, to purchase special privilege in their organic results.

Some telemarketers from authorized resellers will try to tell you they have a distinct say in the way that search results are ranked so they can mark up their prices, but all it shows is that the salespeople don't actually know what AdWords does. A private consulting company like my company has the exact same access to AdWords, so really the margin that comes out of your ad spend isn't getting you anything at all.

Are You Working With a Reseller?

When I'm talking to clients about their past relationships with resellers, there's a line I like to use from the show *Mad Men*: "We're sorry your last girlfriend hurt you."

Most of my clients have had one or more Google AdWords managers in the past who left them with a bad taste in their mouth, either from a lack of tangible results, mediocre campaign performance, or poor service. The best advice I can give you here is that you have to be careful about who is actually working on your behalf.

Honestly ask yourself the following questions: is your service provider someone you can trust to manage your ad spend? Do they understand the ebb and flow of your industry? Where are their profits coming from?

And by the way, if you are currently in one of these relationships and you are one of the lucky ones getting clicks and calls, you're probably paying way too much or missing out on a much larger market opportunity. How do I know that? Because *the performance metrics don't lie*. I've watched as negligent and downright malicious reseller companies have raised their pricing by charging tremendous monthly rates that require you to raise your ad spend to compensate for the margins they are taking from it. When you look at an actual ad spend without all of that opportunity-wasting negligence and outrageous marking-up, you'll see a finely-tuned, closely monitored, and sharply strategic budget maintained with smarter bids and swifter adjustments – a hands-on optimization that the monolithic national companies do not and *cannot* provide. It's time to trim the fat.

Our mismanaged-AdWords advertiser isn't a bad business owner – he just didn't realize that he was being taken advantage of, since the Google reseller seemed completely legitimate and was even authorized by Google to make that sale. How was he supposed to know? Besides, national sales teams are specifically trained to convince you that what you need is what they have.

But you don't need a national or international sales company to manage your PPC. You don't need to be one business in a sea of clients with no identity other than a net profit for a reseller. You don't need a Yodle, a Reach Local, a Dex Media, or a Yellow Pages to handle your AdWords. You don't need another bad relationship that doesn't bring in calls or improve your Google standing. You need:

- A quantifiable return on your investment.

- An account manager who knows your business and doesn't take his revenue from your ad spend.

- A company that keeps track of the most important numbers, the need-to-know success metrics that show what ads are working and what ads are not so you can adjust.

You need...well, you need what the *successful* AdWords advertiser got!

Having just read this section about all of the ways that you and so many other small and medium sized business owners are cheated by reseller fraud and negligent policies, you're probably pretty bummed out, not to mention angry with the status quo.

But some businesses like yours do manage to make their AdWords work, and in the next section I'd like to show you how it's done.

2.3 - The Swimmers

Over on the other side of the pond, you've got the successful AdWords advertiser who knows what a concentrated PPC effort can do for a company.

His cost per call is way below what his competitors are paying, and his AdWords campaigns are optimized to bring in calls with the best possible return on investment. Each of his pay-per-click campaigns is built out accurately and managed precisely by a small team of dedicated professionals using state-of-the-art tracking technology. His cost per click is low because he doesn't have to pay a margin on his ad spend – instead, he pays a flat rate for a comprehensive service level agreement, and he has a full service guarantee without a binding contract. Now he has ads that are proven to convert, call counts that are steadily high and rising, and an AdWords account operating at maximum cost-efficiency and performance.

And guess what? I can tell you exactly how he began.

Need-to-Know Performance Metrics

The successful Google AdWords advertisers of the world always start by making sure that their PPC managers are tracking, adjusting for, and keeping them updated on the following metrics for success. We defined these in our "Google Lexicon," but now let's start to see them in action. AdWords "swimmers" always know their numbers, and they know how to account for losses and gains in ways that push the needle on ad budget and drive up their incoming lead count. If you're going to be like the AdWords swimmer this year, you need minute-to-minute updates on the following:

- **Conversion** – Your website's percentage of click conversion (also known as "conversion rate") is the most critical metric available – and many Google AdWords resellers don't even actually track it! Conversion translates to the number of clicks on your PPC ads that are, in turn, developing into high quality leads. If your current PPC manager tells you how much web traffic you're getting but not how much of that traffic is turning into calls, you need to get out!

- **Website Traffic** – Of course, you need to measure how many people are finding your ads and viewing your site. However, you also need to know that not every click that your ads get is necessarily good. Sometimes, competitors will search and click on your ads to drive up your bid costs, waste your budget, skew your numbers, and learn how to beat your strategy. Other times, spammers will visit your site repeatedly with no intention of ordering service or purchasing your products. Knowing how to distinguish between the different types of web traffic is a learned skill, and a valuable one for making sure that your advertising budget never goes to waste.

- **Call Quality** – Let's say you have a low-quality lead. A prospective customer calls you, but doesn't have the right information – for example, they might be from outside of your service area. If you use a call service, you might never hear about it. But wouldn't you like to see why some calls aren't becoming leads? You should always have the opportunity to listen to your recorded calls. A reseller may record your calls for you, but they'll rarely ever update you when a call goes south. You need management that includes monitoring your calls, letting you know when something goes wrong, and changing your strategy so you only get the best leads – the customers, clients and patients you want.

- **Keyword Optimization** – What are the most searched terms relevant to your business? Does your PPC manager know? If you're working with a national sales team as your AdWords expert, they probably don't understand your industry well enough to preempt the keywords that your business needs to rank for. The result is wasted budget on keywords that don't drive quality leads and revenue. A good PPC company pursues long-tail keywords that yield visible results. We'll discuss more about what that means later on.

The Importance of a Relationship

The difference between the advertiser who failed this year and the advertiser who succeeded was the relationship they had with their AdWords management provider. When you run a small business, you often can't afford the time or energy required to master Google AdWords. Instead, you need to be focused on your clients, so you'll outsource your internet marketing and AdWords campaign management, at least in part.

But while you're focusing on your own clients, customers, and patients, you need an account manager who is focused on *you*.

You need a company who:

- Has a *person* managing your account, so you're not just some string of code in an algorithm (or a net profit on someone's P&L).

- Specializes in your industry, so that you get calls from the customers you want – not just the customers who were easiest to get to.

- Knows who you are and will pick up the phone if you call with a problem.

- Is looking for a *long-term partnership*, not a 3-12 month contract, so you can feel confident that they're with you for the long-haul. Ideally, you won't have to sign on for any minimum time frame in a binding contract at all – that way the guarantees aren't cancelled out by the fine print.

- Values retention over sales, so you know that the employees you work with are trained for PPC service, not just in how to sell the product.

- Offers the technologies you need to convert at higher rates and eliminate wasted budget.

So now I've shown you the horror story, and I've shown you the success story. We've seen real-life examples of the stark differences in PPC coverage between businesses. You now know the *Tale of Two Google AdWords Advertisers*, you know who sank and who swam, and you know why.

Look, you don't need to deal with a massive, international, publicly traded company to do AdWords right. You don't need to pay huge mark-ups for bad service. All you need is a solid relationship with a company who *knows who you are and what you need to do* to make AdWords work for you. Want to learn how to get one of those?

Then keep reading.

BONUS RESOURCES FOR "WHEN PPC SHARKS ATTACK"

Get The How To Hire a Google AdWords Advertising Manager Worksheet ($97 value):

This comprehensive worksheet includes the 21 essential interview questions you need to ask AdWords manager candidates to see if they are qualified to manage your advertising budget.

Join Pay-Per-Click Prosperity – the place for better Google AdWords performance – and access this resource today.
Go to: payperclickprosperity.com

Chapter 2 Survivor's Summary

This chapter surveyed two hypothetical advertisers. One succeeded with AdWords this year by applying the best practices of PPC management relationships, and the other failed due to having a reseller negligently steering his account.

Here we learned about some Google AdWords reseller practices that have hurt small business owners looking to succeed locally with pay-per-click search marketing. First, we did our background research: Steve told us the history of the AdWords reseller program and gave us a definition of resellers that we could work with. We investigated some of the "partnerships" between Google and these sales companies as well as the "5 Lies Google Resellers Will tell You." This information will help you recognize the bad management models that take advantage of your business and fail to produce results.

Next, we did our research: Steve dug into some examples of resellers who have been known to mismanage small business owners' accounts. These included ReachLocal, Yodle, Dex Media, and Yellow Pages.

Finally, we described the properly managed "swimmer" PPC account. You used this opportunity to compare their experience to your own.

Your takeaways from this chapter should be how to spot negligent PPC management practices, how to know if you are working with a reseller, and how a positive PPC relationship is defined.

Test Your Survival Skills: *(Find answers on page 190)*

1. Between 2012 and 2014, advertisers saw a _____% increase on what businesses paid per click through Google AdWords.

2. Not having transparency into your _____ is a serious warning sign that you are working with a negligent reseller.

3. The publicly traded reseller company ReachLocal has been known to place _____% mark-ups on AdWords clicks.

4. Yodle is an international reseller that primarily offers _____ contracts.

In this part, we reviewed the basics of pay-per-click and established the right parameters for a PPC management relationship. You grabbed hold of the lifesaver, and Steve pulled you onto dry land.

So what's next? Well, now you need to set up camp! In Part II, we'll gather all of the resources we need to survive in the Google AdWords wild.

Our primary focus in Part II will be to answer the following questions:

- **What tools and technologies do I need for PPC management?**

- **How do I write ad copy that attracts quality buyers?**

- **Once a prospect has clicked on my ad, how do I turn them into a lead?**

The next chapter will show you all of the components of a successful ad campaign in depth. We'll build our technology foundation, refine our sales copy, and optimize our landing pages to increase our conversion. We're only just beginning!

PART II: THE 3 SURVIVAL NECESSITIES

Step-By-Step Instructions for How to Prepare
for Google AdWords Success

3 | Building Shelter

The 6 Ways To Increase Lead Volume That Your PPC Manager Doesn't Want You To Know About

3.1 - Laying the Groundwork

NOTE: *Before proceeding, the author and editor want you to know that the following is mainly comprised of technological language, i.e. "geeky tech talk." If that sort of thing isn't for you, feel free to take me on my word for this and skip right to the next chapter.*

If you want to survive in the wild, you're going to need to set up a home base. You need a roof over your head that can protect you from the elements! Shelter is one of the fundamental necessities for survival, and now that we've reached dry land, setting up camp is the first thing we need to do.

If you want to succeed with Google AdWords, you're going to need technological support. You need an online web presence that is built to last – that means having security measures and enough fire power in place to protect you from fraudulent activity and site malfunctions. In this section, I'm going to teach you how to construct your technological "shelter" in the Google AdWords wild to help you protect and organize your account. Proper shelter is key to survival, and having the right technology is integral to success in the modern marketing world.

The simple fact of the matter is that other businesses in the internet marketing industry don't invest in technology the same way I do. Your small business competitors will not have the same server platforms used by Fortune 500 Companies. AdWords Resellers will not go to extreme lengths to file click fraud claims and get ad spend refunds from Google…in fact, they often *profit* from click fraud since they still receive cost margins from those clicks. Still, many people will say what I do is overkill and that there are ways to cut corners on technology that keep you at eye level with the competition. However, I'm the type of guy who likes to do things right, and when I put my head on my pillow at night I sleep with a clear conscience – and I know I won't wake up to any problems.

Plus, I'm laughing my way to the bank, because I know that superior technology has the *best return on investment in the PPC game.* We're all using Google AdWords, so some might say that the playing field is level – but I know better than that from experience. I've seen companies whose websites tanked from having shared servers that crashed for days with no back-ups, all while their AdWords campaigns were still running. I've seen people lose their ad positioning from a lack of intelligence reporting, sluggish adjustment to market trends, and outright ignorance of budget-bleeding browser incompatibilities. I've seen Google refunds of hundreds of dollars for one month of click fraud – money that most AdWords users never see, simply because their PPC managers don't want to put in the effort. But that's the sort of effort that matters, and it all starts with having the right tools, the proper infrastructure, and a team that cares.

What do the right tools look like? To me, your survival shelter looks like this:

Website

You would think that just about every company nowadays would have a website, right? After all, with rates of online search going through the roof, you'd need to capitalize on the more than 80% of consumers who research online before making large purchases[32] – and a website in the central hub of a functional web presence! Of course, since 4 out of 5 of businesses claim to have a web presence,[33] you'd think they must have a website… right?

But you'd unfortunately be wrong. As of October of 2013, nearly half of small-to-medium businesses had no company website at all – and only 6% of SMBs currently have a site optimized for mobile devices![34]

To me, what this proves is that the majority of companies don't understand the sheer rate of acceleration happening in the online marketing world. If you're one step behind on your web presence one year, you're ten steps behind for the next! Since 2009, mobile devices have achieved the following:

The Statistics of Mobile Search[35]

- Tripled share of online media consumption (now 12% of web browsing is facilitated through a smartphone).

- Increased rate of mobile purchases by over 15%.

- Have been used for online shopping by nearly two-thirds of mobile owners.

- Accounted for 19% of Google's ad revenue…that number is growing, and it's not likely to start losing steam!

Why is this important?

Every site that I've ever built for my clients has been device-responsive: that means the pages can automatically resize their layout based on the device they are being viewed from, whether that's a tablet, a smartphone, or a desktop computer. To me, wasted opportunities are money out the window. Your online presence's marketing potential isn't complete until it's accessible from *all relevant media.*

Mobile is projected to drive *50% of paid search clicks by 2015.*[36] And yet, less than 10% of small business owners have mobile responsive sites! It's a staggering oversight that's going to play a major role in the success and failure of SMBs in the next year. Mobile search is an opportunity for businesses that is quite literally growing by the minute – are you going to capitalize, or let your PPC manager sit back while those crucial moments slip by? This is where being ahead of the game in technological investment becomes a difference of dollars and cents.

In addition, I always have my clients' sites built on a user-friendly content management system (CMS) like WordPress to allow us to make changes easily. Why? Because your business isn't a static entity. As you grow, your content should change. Intuitive CMS providers make the editing process quick and painless. Why grapple with HTML when you can manage your website without having to speak a coding language?

The next step to having a truly dynamic website is looking into a process known as "caching." One common analogy for caching is grocery shopping, since the basic concept is the same. Just like you buy groceries from the store so that you have all of the ingredients you need in one place, your website takes material from a larger access point for more readily available storage in the cache. Think of your web cache as being like your kitchen cabinets. They store the products that aren't in use for easy access later. Obviously, you wouldn't buy a cup of flour from the grocery store every time you needed it in a recipe – you buy enough so that you can make many meals without requiring a return trip. In the same way, your web cache stores page information that can be used for more efficient retrieval in the future, that way you don't have to keep fetching the same information over and over. This optimizes performance and eliminates lag, making for smoother and smarter page viewing. In fact, web caching can be the difference between a 1 second page load time and a 60 second page load time – that's a pretty enormous difference in user experience! All of this guarantees that your prospective customers feel comfortable and encouraged to buy from your company's site or stay on the page and call you for service.

Finally, your website needs a means of built-in lead tracking. That means that you'll need call-tracking software that tells you exactly what landing pages on your website are bringing in leads, that way you can adjust your ad spend according to the success of those pages.

This is where having a "microsite" built out can be useful. Microsites are service-specific domains attached to your main URL. For instance, if you own a plumbing company and a large percentage of your revenue comes from drain cleaning and repair, you may want a drain specific microsite. If your main site's URL is "www.callpaulsplumbing.com," your microsite would be something like "drains.callpaulsplumbing.com."

Moreover, you also need lead-capture forms for your landing pages, because what's the point of a landing page if it's not getting any information about your leads? Ideally, built-in form-capture provides a simple and appealing outlet for customers to enter their contact information.

So ask yourself these questions in this order:

- Does my company have a functioning website?
- Is that website responsive to mobile and tablet views?
- Can I change the content on my site easily?
- Does it optimize user experience by caching (i.e. reducing lag)?
- Does it take advantage of built-in call-tracking?
- Does it take advantage of built-in form-capture to capture leads?

Until you can answer yes to all of these questions, you can't honestly say your web presence is optimized for advertising. Any PPC budget that you do have will experience at least some degree of waste, since not all the possible capacities for improving conversion are actually in use. Harsh, I know – but true.

But even then, a well designed website is only part one of the technology you need! A great site means nothing if it's sitting on a crashed server.

Server Foundation

Do you think that the largest and most successful companies in the U.S. have their multi-million dollar websites sitting on a GoDaddy server? Nothing against GoDaddy – but of course not. Those companies don't settle for cheap alternatives, they want the best. They don't just buy prime server technology because they can afford it, either – they do it because it offers them the protection and competitive edge they need to continue dominating their market. Don't get me wrong: I'm a great GoDaddy customer with more than 500 domains in my portfolio, plus I love their Superbowl commercials as much as the next guy. However, when it comes to server security, theirs is not the route to success.

Server technology is just like anything else in that *you get what you pay for*. You might buy a sandwich at the gas station if you're hungry and in a hurry, but you don't expect a gourmet meal. You might even anticipate that your stomach won't like you very much in a couple of hours. But unlike Turkey Club a la Shell Station, a bad server can put *all of your business and financial assets at risk*. Server technology is not a purchase, it's an investment – and making a poor investment in this area will spell disaster should anything go wrong.

But what *can* go wrong? I'll show you what I mean. A low quality community server can:

- Go down for days, weeks, months, and even permanently if anything happens to the technology. In the time that it takes you to diagnose and repair the hang-up, you could be losing thousands of dollars in potential sales and missed opportunity.

- Put you at risk of Quality Score penalization if Google finds someone else on your shared server practicing marketing strategies that violate their terms of service.

- Result in longer-than-average wait times for people who click on your ads. What would you do if you clicked on an ad only to find that the website was going to take 30 seconds to load? That's right: you probably wouldn't even know it took 30 seconds at all, since you'd hit the back button after one third of that time!

- Leave you and your customers vulnerable to site hackers and identity thieves.

Most AdWords managers don't invest in server hardware. That technology is not their prerogative. In the event of failure, you'll have no one to turn to, since your PPC point-of-contact will only take the crash as an opportunity to point fingers at someone else for your sluggish numbers – and good luck finding an employee at GoDaddy who's willing to take accountability for a community server going down!

That's just another factor that makes my business model different. I invest in my clients *from the ground up.* That means starting their website on a dedicated server with the following features:

- Dynamic DNS, meaning we host your site on a server that changes the name server address in case of failure, so all of your traffic is simply rerouted to a backup and nothing is lost. This happens automatically in the event of a crash in my camp.

- Built-in redundancy. We run paid search websites on two concurrent servers in case one of them should ever crash, so your site will never be down.

- Fast servers with the best processors in the field, so your site will have the memory and performance to optimize user experience.

- Active real-time server performance monitoring.

- Complete control to give you fast troubleshooting, accurate solutions, and total security all year long.

Can I guarantee that you'll experience a server failure if you use a cheap community server? Not necessarily. But I can absolutely guarantee that you'll wish you'd made the investment if it ever happens! In fact, I can say with total confidence that your revenue for the entire year can be thrown off by a single server incident.

How do I know? It's happened to me.

Way back when I was a one-man band and managed accounts from my tiny apartment, I relied on my clients to go out and purchase their own hardware. I learned the importance of server security early on the hard way. I spent many sleepless nights helping clients out of failed server relationships. As my company has matured to the marketing & technology business it is today, I can proudly say I haven't had a server incident in quite some time.

Server failure is one of the most expensive disasters that can happen to a company, and what are you paying your current PPC guy for if not some security in the ever-shifting world of online marketing? It's a survival necessity! You either shell out for the proper equipment, or you leave yourself exposed to the elements. Before you ask yourself if you can afford a server upgrade, ask if you can afford to risk losing everything over night or having your ads shut down for days.

Once you've got your site set on the right server, then you can turn your full attention to how many leads your site is bringing you. As I've already said, the rate at which the traffic to your landing pages becomes actual client leads is known as "conversion," and it's critical to keep your site conversion healthy. However, there are some clicks your ads will receive that are never going to become leads – simply because these viewers were never intending to make the purchase. This brings us to our next prerequisite technology for AdWords management:

Click Fraud Protection

Click fraud is a bit of a "dirty little secret" in the PPC industry – but don't be fooled by its low profile, because click fraud can literally cost you hundreds, if not thousands, in a single month, and it probably already has. The definition is as follows, with phrasing taken directly from Google itself:

⚙ **Click fraud** – a term for both clicks and impressions on AdWords ads that are not the result of genuine user interest. This covers intentionally fraudulent traffic as well as accidental clicks and other mechanically generated traffic.

I see companies suffer from click fraud all the time. Frequently, the source is a competitor trying to figure out your strategies, drive up your spend, and take you out of the game by exhausting your daily budget. Click fraud can result in huge chunks of your ad spend being completely wasted.

But not when you're my client.

That's because I have built a proprietary click fraud protection software solution we use internally for all of the accounts we manage. This allows me and my team to track site visitors by their IP addresses and monitor their behavior. If I see suspicious activity, I can tag them as a potential threat. If the suspicious activity continues, I can block their IP address from viewing your ads. The ads simply won't show on their Google searches, meaning your budget isn't charged for advertising that isn't going to be effective. I can even make your website invisible to them so competitors looking to get intelligence on your business are stopped in their tracks. It's like having a full-time private investigator always holding your site performance under a magnifying glass in the search for bad clicks that cost you money without bringing it back in.

And here's where it gets really good: I can report click fraud to Google in order to receive refunds on malicious click activity. With the proper documentation, which I attain from the recorded system of checks and balances supplied by our technology, I can successfully make the case that my clients' cost per click was manipulated unfairly, which results in Google writing them a check. Through this extra step, I've won hundreds of dollars back for clients who, with previous PPC managers, had no idea why their bid costs were so high.

This is a service that you will never get from an AdWords manager who does not have this technology. These steps require your PPC manager to know your company, track every single click, have vested interest in a long term relationship with your business, and be willing to go the extra mile to prevent even the most insidious forms of ad spend waste – not to mention the fact that you need to have the right tools. But it's all one and the same in the end, because if your PPC manager doesn't have this kind of software already, they've already proven that they don't meet those other criteria. They aren't willing to invest in your success.

Bottom line is this: being able to achieve and maintain a certain degree of website traffic is a relatively simple matter of investing time and money. Getting the conversion rates of your PPC ads to consistently beat your competitors is a matter of *skill*. Developing that skill starts with having access to resources like click fraud protection software to help you eliminate waste. Our conversion-driven approach means more inbound calls for your business – which leads me to the next piece of your AdWords foundation that we need to discuss:

Call-Tracking Technology

If you aren't tracking your calls, then you have no idea how well your PPC campaigns are going. Calls are the lifeblood of any business with customers, clients, or patients, and it's why I'm picky about who I work with: I'll do the footwork that gets you calls, but you've got to be there to pick up the phone. I can't answer calls for you, and I can't force a prospect to give you their credit card information, but there are some things I can do to make your calls better and more contributive to the overall performance of your sales funnel.

> **1. Reviewing Call Quality** – All of the calls I bring in are recorded for quality. Then a member from my team listens to those recordings to pick out the issues – for instance, if an ad is miscommunicating an idea or if calls are coming from outside of your service area. From there, I can quickly diagnose and fix the problem.

> To manually listen to the entire call volume of a small business is

time-consuming, but I've found it to be worth the effort, especially early on in a relationship. There's a good chance your current PPC company is not doing this, which means mistakes can go undetected for days, weeks, and even months. Customers, clients, and patients can be going to your after-hours answering service and hanging up because your automated message is too long, and you would never know. By identifying dropped calls and lost opportunities, you're able to catch problems before they start.

The ability to catch problems before they severely impact your budget is just one of the many incentives for having someone monitor your calls.

You also need to record calls because reviewing them will allow you to calculate their approximate value (as per the service being ordered), giving you a better estimate of the return on your investment. In addition, recorded calls are helpful for training your call takers to improve their overall performance.

2. Routing to Unique Numbers – Let's say you create two landing pages. You'll want to know how well each page is converting. If they each have the direct phone number to your call center, how will you know which landing pages are bringing in calls?

If you want to split-test ad copy, branch out on your offers, or even just run two separate campaigns at once, you'll need the ability to individually assign call-tracking numbers to each landing page. With the technology I use, a multitude of combinations are possible. You can:

- Forward all different numbers to the same call center.
- Have some landing pages that split calls 50/50 between numbers.
- Time your calls so that, if one phone doesn't pick up after a certain number of rings, the call is passed to the next number.
- Make multiple phones ring at once.

The ability to create distinct phone numbers for each campaign you create is critical to performance tracking and efficiently managing the calls that my PPC advice is going to be bringing in – not to mention how it will protect your revenue and ability to create new opportunities.

3. Local Area Codes – This one is pretty straightforward. You need the ability to purchase local phone numbers for your campaigns. That way, customers don't balk at the sight of a generic 800 number that they think could be connecting them to any location in the U.S. In my experience, I have found that local businesses who use a generic 800 number almost always get a lower conversion rate compared to those clients who use numbers with local area codes corresponding to their target cities when targeting local consumers.

All of these tools are just for tracking calls. However, as you know already, there are a number of other critical metrics to keep a pulse on, and how effectively and consistently you do so will have a major impact on the success of your campaigns. That's why you need...

Real-Time Performance Scorecard

Question: with your current PPC company, do you receive an email at the end of each day telling you exactly how many calls you received? You should! Or how about an automated email every time the phone rings? You can!

As I've said already, the PPC game needs to be played in real-time – that means making updates as they come so you can make adjustments as they're needed. If you're going about your week just hoping your PPC manager is doing what they're supposed to do, chances are that you're not getting the attention your company needs. Someone needs to be there and be held accountable for your PPC performance at all times.

Your business needs a ticker-tape. Stock market analogies of your call-tracking, cost per click, conversion, and the other need-to-know performance metrics allow you to clearly and intuitively see where your PPC campaigns are working properly and where they need improvement. They allow your PPC manager to control your AdWords bids more effectively and fine-tune your ads to be lead-generating machines.

Having an "AdWords tickertape" will help your account thrive – however, to be honest, I'm not so keen on the "tickertape" comparison. Even though it does fit the bill, I'd like to use an analogy with a bit more warmth. So here's another one:

Recently (as I'm putting the finishing touches on this book, in fact), I just had a baby girl. Well, not me personally – all of the credit there goes to my wife, Allison. At the hospital in the labor and delivery room, we waited almost 24 hours for our precious daughter, Madeline Rose, to come into this world. It was a stressful day, to say the least.

All the while, my wife's belly was hooked up to a baby heart monitor. The monitor would track each and every beat, notifying the doctor and nurses of any irregular or out-of-the-ordinary rhythms. And let me tell you something – something you might already know if you have children of your own – I saw *every single heartbeat* come across that screen. Thankfully, Madeline was born completely healthy, and being a father is incredible – but you're crazy if you think the doctor was going to know about an irregular heart rhythm before me.

Now, imagine if you had a heart monitor strapped up to your campaigns. Would you watch it every second, like my wife and I did for our firstborn? Well, maybe not quite as closely as that. But I think my point still stands: your business is your baby, and we always want to make sure our babies are safe. You need technology that will keep a pulse on your AdWords 24/7.

That's why all of my intelligence reporting comes at real-time pace. There's no time for lag when your company has money on the line.

Quit dealing with the lackluster reports, the half-truth numbers, and the outright failure to communicate. Start playing the AdWords game like you're in it to win.

That means showing up with best equipment on the market. It means being prepared in every possible way and seeing what the competition doesn't see. It means having a PPC manager who has the right tools and knows how to use them to make you successful.

Let me show you what I mean.

3.2 - Introducing ClickOptix

I'm sure you're a bit dizzy by now, but I promise the geek section of this *Survival Guide* is almost over. I hope I've hit home how extremely important it is for a PPC manager to be able to access his technology infrastructure. Before we move on to the next critical step of AdWords survival, I want to share one more item I've got on my utility belt to give you a better sense of how I come to every ad campaign prepared for absolutely anything.

There's one more moving part to our technology systems: it's called ClickOptix, and it's a software we've built to monitor the heartbeat of your successful Google AdWords campaign. It is the solution my team and I use internally, and we give all of our clients access to it so that they can see their real-time business performance data.

With ClickOptix, you're able to see everything, track everything, improve conversions, and estimate waste.

We'll talk in more detail later on about how my team actually works. Our approach to account management is one-of-a-kind, and I want to give you a full behind-the-scenes look – you'll also see more specifics in the resources included at the end of this chapter.

But for now, I wanted to take this opportunity to give my best technology its due credit. ClickOptix is a software solution that pulls in real-time performance data from our call-tracking, from Google Analytics, and from Google AdWords, and then combines these numbers onto one spreadsheet so we know exactly how our clients are performing up to the minute. Picture, if you will, a stock ticker – or a heart monitor – on a large screen in our office. Our client accounts scroll by in a rolling rotation, and my PPC specialists are able to react immediately to changes in both market conditions and account performance. We track all of the mission critical data that makes our accounts so successful, including daily market traffic, number of clicks, lead conversions, cost per call, budget, daily spend, and click fraud. We feed all of this data to a single location and use it to forecast how our clients are going to end up at the end of the month.

ClickOptix lets us benchmark similar clients against each other. For example, all of our plumbers across the country are averaged out in real-time, and we are able to quickly identify when there is a company not in alignment with our national averages. For clients that have been with me for a while, we are also able to benchmark their performance against historical data and work toward achieving better numbers month over month.

At the end of each business day, we use this tool to print out our daily "redlines" report, which identifies all of our accounts that need immediate attention.

We provide our clients with access to this information so they can log in and see their account reporting on-demand at any point throughout the course of the day or week. Back in the old days, we would tally up performance and print out reports for our clients at the end of the month. Changes were slow to come, and you didn't always catch in-month alterations to market conditions such as increased traffic, decreased traffic, weather events, increases or decreases in competitors' bids, new competitor ad copy, changes in mobile bids, drops in ad placement, surges in ad placement, rising click costs, falling click costs, competitors who drop out of the game, and so on and so forth.

The ClickOptix system gives us a read on your market and helps us make daily changes to your account to improve performance. It's an extremely powerful business intelligence tool, and I consider it one of our core differentiators in the marketplace. Thanks to ClickOptix data, we get a black and white picture of an account's status at any given moment to help us make decisions on behalf of our clients.

To request a demo, go to ClickOptix.com.

If your PPC manager is still shuffling around reports and emailing them to you at the end of the month, it won't be long before both of you are falling behind. You most likely are calling him frequently to tell him things have slowed down or you've experienced a dip in performance. What I'm saying on my end is that, with ClickOptix, you don't even need to call to tell us how great your numbers look – we already know.

BONUS RESOURCES FOR "BUILDING YOUR SHELTER"

Register Now for this Webinar On-Demand ($297 value): *Setting the Foundation For Google AdWords Success: 5 Step-By-Step Ways To Capture More Opportunities Using The Right Technology.* This webinar will give you a clear picture of how wasted advertising spend can be avoided, how to generate more leads, and how to implement a competitive edge that will take your market by surprise. You will learn:

1. How you can track your ROI with the right call-tracking tool.

2. How you can capture the growing amount of mobile prospects with the right responsive website.

3. How you can reduce wasted ad spend and eliminate click fraud once and for all.

4. How you can get a bird's eye view of real-time performance metrics that will help you steer the Google AdWords ship.

Join Pay-Per-Click Prosperity – the place for better Google AdWords performance – and access this resource today.
Go to: payperclickprosperity.com

Chapter 3 Survivor's Summary

In this chapter, we introduced the 5 most important tools and technologies to have at your disposal when running Google AdWords PPC.

Your takeaways from this chapter should be how your site is hosted and how to keep track of critical performance metrics.

Test Your Survival Skills: *(Find answers on page 190)*

1. Mobile search is projected to drive _____ % of paid search clicks in 2015.

2. The term for clicks on AdWords ads that are not the result of genuine user interest is _____.

4

Hunting Your Food

Discover How to Uncover Your Prospects' Pain and Turn Them Into New Customers, Clients or Patients Following These 10 Killer Ad Copy Rules.

4.1 - Knowing Your Ideal Customer

As soon as you've carved out some shelter for yourself, it's time to start hunting.

Only you aren't hunting prey — you're targeting a demographic. Your ad copy is your weapon, and you need to know how to shape it and wield it to bring the revenue home. How can you run a Google AdWords marketing campaign without knowing how to write ads? You'd have just about as much of a chance as you would trying to survive in the wild with no source of food.

Most PPC management is technical in nature. As we learned in the last chapter, a solid third of what makes up a successful AdWords campaign is bringing the correct tools to the table. Given enough time and money, anyone can setup a webpage and drive traffic to it — however, it takes an intimate understanding of your target client, along with some constructive marketing experience, to convert traffic to leads that result in revenue.

Even if resellers, upsellers, and weak Pay-Per-Call branded websites (i.e. a simple site that a phone book publisher would throw up for you) were backing your account with the right technology, it still wouldn't be enough to truly make those campaigns succeed — but they'll still try! Beware the

AdWords manager who tries to use software to create and manage ad copy. For copy to be effective, it has to be a manual process.

Use people, not machines, when it comes to ad copy.

Writing truly great ad copy, the second necessity of AdWords survival, requires dedication, time commitment, and expertise to work properly. Here's why:

> *Technology is important, but computers can't do everything: about 30% of marketing automation customers reported unsatisfactory lead generation rates in 2014.*[37]

1. **Dedication and Time Commitment** – Effort and hard work will increase your conversion. A winning strategy in managing ad copy includes testing – rigorous, disciplined testing. With machines, there's no effort being applied, and in the rapidly paced world of Google AdWords, automation means a lack of attention. You might have noticed that most (if not all) of the technology foundation components I mentioned require some degree of monitoring. That's because without a real person performing checks and making adjustments, you've got nobody steering the ship! And I don't know about you, but I'm not exactly rushing out to buy one of Google's driverless cars just yet. I'll keep my eyes on the road, thank you very much.

2. **Expertise** – I'm about to show you the secrets that make ad copy succeed. Still, though, even these secret techniques were learned over many years of research, experience, and good ol' fashioned trial and error. Great ad copy isn't built in a day. It requires focus and knowledge to really make it work.

So what kind of knowledge am I talking about? I don't mean strategies, because the winning strategies are exactly what I'm about to tell you. Just by reading this book, you will have already come that far. No, it's a very specific sort of knowledge that I'm referring to here, and it's what you need to start with whenever you set yourself to writing new ad copy for a PPC campaign: I'm talking about intimate knowledge of your potential customer's problems.

Understanding Your Prospect's Pain

All of that geeky tech stuff from last chapter is over now. Here's where the marketing begins!

When you sit down and start to develop ads for your market, the first question you need to ask yourself is this: "Who is my ideal customer, client, or patient?" Getting to know your market is one thing, but getting to know the precise profile of who you want to sell to is another thing altogether. Taking the time to get to know your prospects on a personal level will set you apart from the competition – you'll be going in the total opposite direction of what everybody else is doing.

And that's a good thing! In most competitive local markets, ads are very similar because no one is actually applying these principles. The typical marketing game becomes a question of "Who can spend the most money to plaster the world and the internet with ads?" In many instances, this results in the little guy getting trampled by larger franchise companies who can afford massive marketing departments. But when you introduce principled ad copy, you change the game completely. Then it becomes not an issue of how much advertising you can buy, but how well you can market. And that's when you start to pull ahead of the pack.

The winning formula for AdWords ad copy has all of these ingredients:

1. Anticipation of the prospect's needs.
2. Knowledge of the economics behind the product or service being sold.
3. Research into the keywords that people are searching.
4. Testing of ad copy to see how the market reacts.

When you put all of these pieces together, you get a picture of the person you're trying to market to: a synopsis of your Ideal Prospect.

Let's go over the different types of customers in general terms. We'll talk about three in particular, and we'll describe them using a simple graphic I call the "Buyer's Triangle." There are three primary qualities that define a consumer's search, and they constitute the three points:

Buyer's Triangle

The three questions to ask yourself about your Ideal Prospect, are:

• At what level is the prospect's demand (i.e. what's their degree of urgency? How fast do they need your product or service)?

• What price are they willing to pay?

• How much are they going to research and kick tires before they decide to buy?

You can form a pretty decent idea of how your customer behaves by using this simple diagram. We're going to construct three distinct buyer profiles using the sides of this triangle. Keep in mind, these profiles are fairly general…but you're going to see how true they are across every possible market and service in just a moment as I break it down for you.

The "Give It to Me Now" High Demand/High Price Range Persona

When the customer, client or patient looking for your service has a high level of urgency and a high price range, they fall into the "Give It to Me Now" character bracket. This is the kind of customer who goes online thinking, "I don't even care how much it costs, I need this fixed ASAP!" or "I've got to have XYZ right now!" These are the prospects whom you need to be hitting with your PPC. The whole point of having a Google AdWords account is so that when somebody goes online and types in your specific service, they wind up finding your ad. The "Give It to Me Now" customer is a huge part of the reason that PPC is important: you need to be there when those customers, clients and patients are online and trying to track you down!

EXAMPLE: An overweight heart attack patient gets out of the hospital, and their doctor tells them they need to get healthier now or they'll risk having another incident. Now this customer wants an appointment with a weight loss physician pronto, and they're willing to pay whatever it costs to get the attention they need to fix their problem.

Now, you may be thinking that this kind of customer is fairly rare, since emergency situations are – by definition – not the norm. Of course, life-and-death scenarios aren't exactly common. You might even think that your particular service doesn't have a high-demand/high-price range customer to target. But I'm here to tell you that the exact opposite is true.

Every market has this type of customer, client, or patient. The potential to advertise to high demand/high price prospects exists for every business model. You just need to know how to look.

For instance, let's say that you're an accountant. You might think being a CPA means that business is consistent, straightforward, or even boring – but there are tax emergencies, and they happen every day.

A small business owner has two primary fears: bankruptcy and the IRS. In fact, those two fears frequently walk hand in hand! When the owner of a basic storefront does his payroll accounting on a software like Intuit Payroll or the like, they rely on the makers of that software to get their numbers in on time. But what if something goes wrong? Well, the small business owner gets a letter from the IRS. Even though he knows he paid on time, the letter says he's being fined for being two days late. Getting in his taxes on a Thursday when they were due on Tuesday can result in a fine of over $1,000 for this hypothetical business owner. Imagine if he was a month late! If he doesn't have a CPA, the first thing he's going to do is get online and start looking for tax help.

You can also find emergencies in service contractor industries. When a homeowner discovers a sewer backup pushing into their home, they want a solution *now*. When someone's heating dies in the dead of winter and they need a furnace repair, they're going to want it repaired *today*. When an outlet in somebody's house explodes, they need rewiring *straight away*. They're going to look for plumbers, HVAC installers, and electricians in their area online by clicking through the first ads. The first guy to pick up the phone gets the sale.

So it's really not just medical emergencies that can capitalize on "Give It To Me Now" scenarios. Every market has a pocket of high demand. In order to reach these customers, your ad copy needs to address real, obvious pain. You need to preempt the pressing issues that can occur in your field and be the one who arrives first at the scene. The "Give It to Me Now" customer is an invaluable asset, so ask yourself:

- What are the high demand/high price range scenarios in my business?

- How can I speak to them in a way that addresses their problem more directly than any of my competitors?

We're going to get around to addressing that second question more in-depth right after we finish discussing all of the different potential types of customers. Rest assured, though, that it's going to involve ad copy that emphasizes speed and a strategy that stresses visibility. Emergency situations (hopefully) are not a big part of your own life, but what you need to realize is that, as a marketer trying to reach a wider audience, there are emergencies happening every single day. For the people in these scenarios, price is normally not an issue – what matters to them is convenience and expediency. To truly maximize your success, your business and your ad copy need to be a part of addressing those emergency situations with prompt, quality care.

The "Value-Driven" Low Demand/ Mid Price Range Persona

At first glance, the "Value-Driven" and the "Give It to Me Now" customers appear to be on near opposite ends of the spectrum. But that doesn't mean they aren't both valuable. I'm including this guy mainly because I want to clear up the common misconception that the "Value-Driven" buyer is not a quality lead. He is – you just need to have the right ad copy!

This customer is defined by a middling degree of urgency: they want your product or service, but they have some hesitations. They also want to feel reassured they are getting the best possible value for the money they are about to part with.

Now, some business models take this as an opportunity to drop their prices to the point where they're barely making any return off of a purchase. But that's not the way to go. Remember, there will always be somebody out there who is willing to go lower than you. Grocery store owners, you've got your Wal-Mart. Auto-mechanics, you've got your PepBoys. Service contractors, you've got your fly-by-nighters. Besides, the "Value-Driven" prospect isn't going to buy a mediocre product just because it has "SALE" on the price-tag. The leads who do *that* aren't worth your time. Price-sensitive and "Value-Driven" shoppers are often confused for one another, but they aren't the same: your "Value-Driven" customers, clients, and patients aren't *cheap*, they just want to be sure they're getting a solid deal.

No, the key isn't lower prices. Let's take another look at our Buyer's Triangle.

If we look at the full profile of the "Value-Driven" lead, it reads like this: Low Demand/Mid Price Range/*High Degree of Research*. The "Mid Price Range" doesn't mean they aren't willing to pay extra for quality, just that they're willing to search around for better costs before committing.

The "Give It to Me Now" customer's full profile, as you probably guessed, was like this: High Demand/High Price Range/*Low Degree of Research*.

Generally speaking, a client that is likely to make a purchase has two "High" qualities on the Buyer's Triangle I showed you earlier, which means that you need to ramp up another one in the "Value-Driven" profile in order to make them a buyer. The answer, then, lies in generating demand.

The "Value-Driven" lead wants your product or service. But how do you make them *need* it?

Enter AD COPY, stage right.

There are a number of ways you can adjust your ad copy in order to create urgency where it wasn't already. For instance, you can use deadlines. Some of my own clients have been very successful using a scaling deadline strategy: you give them, say, a 30% discount on the service if they order before October 31st, a 20% discount if they order by November 30th, and a 10% discount if they order by December 31st. Oh, and by the way, it's a 40% discount if you order online right now. The "Value-Driven" lead realizes that the best values aren't going to lie around and wait forever. You've successfully created immediate demand, high-five!

Another means of creating urgency is to use scarcity. You see it all the time: "Limited supply, order now!" I've found that by using an actual number, you optimize your results. Tell your "Value-Driven" buyer that there are just 2 items left on a particular sale, or that you're only giving away X amount of service opportunities at this low price point.

The third way to generate demand for the "Value-Driven" lead is to run a price-match guarantee. What this does is implement "risk-reversal," which we'll discuss in more detail later on. But for now, let's do some vocab:

⟲   **Risk-Reversal Offer** – a guarantee that grants a customer, client, or patient certainty that they are paying the right price and will receive the product they desire, making them more likely to enter the purchase stage of your sales funnel. It essentially removes the entire element of risk (i.e. no "buyer beware" catches).

Many super-stores across the U.S. use Price-Match guarantees that automatically credit customers for finding a better deal. Obviously, this appeals to the "Value-Driven" consumer, who is, after all, online right now to find the best deals anyway.

And finally, we've come to the best way to create demand for a product: simply *emphasize the pain.* For the hypothetical I mentioned earlier with the "Give It to Me Now" personas, the urgency was built-in to the situation – however, the same sense of urgency can be drummed up without an existent emergency. For instance, if an overweight person doesn't talk to a diet specialist about their weight, they could be at risk of health conditions or even a heart attack. If a small business owner doesn't have a CPA, the IRS could fine them thousands of dollars for mishandled taxes and they'd have nowhere to turn.

The list of possible examples goes on. If you don't get a drain inspection, you could have clogs forming in your pipes that could break your fixtures at any time and allow disease-carrying bacteria into your home. If you don't give your furnace its pre-season tune-up, it could fail in the middle of winter or, worse, emit poisonous carbon monoxide from a cracked heat exchanger. If your house is old, your wiring is probably old too, so you need a safety inspection to prevent potential electrical fires. If you don't schedule that teeth-cleaning procedure, your mouth will be filled with cavities…and so on and so forth.

Statistics, pictures, videos, and testimonials all help. You should be working these things into your ad copy anyway, regardless of what offer approach you choose.

With quality ad copy, you can draw in a large enough percentage of these "Value-Driven" leads that your revenue will cover the cost of the ads and more. That's what smart marketing is all about: casting a sturdy net where you know there are fish. When you do it right, there's really no gambling involved.

Now, I have clients who will tell me that the "Value-Driven" lead is not for them. They even place barriers and obstacles in front of "Value-Driven" searchers to disqualify them from their sales funnel, such as strict "no refund" policies or expensive price quotes. That's perfectly acceptable, and these qualifiers do reduce your volume of overly price-sensitive callers – but if you apply them too liberally, they can cut your lead generation capacity by a third. You'd be surprised by just how many online shoppers fall into the "Value-Driven" category and how many high quality opportunities you lose by counting them out.

I'll give you an example, because I actually just saw one happen in real life.

As I was writing this book – in fact, while I was writing this chapter – I took my wife out to dinner at an upscale seafood restaurant and overheard a fascinating conversation at the table over. The woman behind me was complaining about the plumbing company that charged her an $89 diagnostic fee to install a $99 faucet. She was eating lobster, drinking expensive red wine, and talking about all of the other properties she owned that needed plumbing help!

I'd venture to guess (as I hope you would too) that this woman was not hung up on the price. She would pay top dollar for service, just like we were all paying top dollar for a quality dinner experience. This woman was not on a ramen noodle budget, so why would she care? The fact of the matter is that it wasn't the cost that was throwing her off – she was just hung up on an $89 trip fee. She was in her late fifties, so I assume that a "diagnostics fee" is a relatively new concept for her. Her generation was conditioned to pay service professionals by the hour, so she didn't understand why she was paying an upfront fee before any work had been done. The flat-rate price model was probably not explained to her by the customer service representative who backed the call.

This is a scenario where it's critical to make a distinction between price-sensitive and "Value-Driven." Had this customer understood that she wasn't paying double for the same amount of work, she might have stayed with this plumbing company for her other jobs as well!

You have to take into consideration the LTV, the customer's "Life Time Value," when you're positioning any offer. The "Value-Driven" lead isn't looking for a free lunch – they just want to be a smart buyer! Your ad copy, especially on large ticket items, ought to consider that.

Okay, now let's get serious, because we're about to discuss our most analytical lead. It's all business with this guy – and I know exactly how to get him.

The "Researcher" High Degree of Research/ High Price Range Persona

This lead isn't necessarily your average Joe. "Reseacher" profiles are the teachers, the science people, the folks who read the fine print – these are buyers who like to read the entire iTunes Terms and Conditions before clicking "I Agree." Now, when I say that they are "high price range," I of course don't mean that they're going to pay you outrageous sums of money for just anything. I mean that, proportional to what they make, the price of the item doesn't matter in the same way that the quality and value does. They need the product that you're selling – but that need isn't urgent enough that they're going to call you before they know *exactly* what they're getting.

When dealing with this customer, you've got to put your best "expert" foot first. You need to give them the information they're looking for in a compact and convenient package that leads them to the next stage in the sale. As I'm always one to say, "Give the people what they want!" Develop something of value for your "Researcher" leads to come out for. Something educational that collects their info and forms the foundation of a relationship. Something that effectively positions you as "the authority" in your field.

In order to sell to the "Researcher," you need to gain their trust. That means constructing a longer sales cycle, sure. But it shouldn't mean that you're straining yourself. With the right sales copy and turnkey assets, there are ways to set up a sales funnel for the "Researcher" leads that don't require perpetual reconfiguring. What it takes is just an initial time investment in the ad copy that you're going to use.

These people are looking for third party affirmations, so give them:

- Testimonials.
- Customer Reviews (you should have an easy-to-access review page).
- Product Research from independent third party experts.
- An E-Book Buyer's Guide.
- Reports on the Product.
- Free Sample Kits.

As an example, lets look at SunSetter Awnings. This is a company based out of my home town that does a great job generating leads for custom-installed awnings using direct response advertising strategies. See, the people who purchase SunSetter Awnings don't have an urgent need. It's not a must-have purchase like bread and milk. It's a luxury item for a homeowner who wants to enjoy their deck without the sun in their eyes. The marketers for SunSetter Awnings know their buyer profiles, and they advertise to them strategically. Here's the simple lead funnel they've designed:

- They advertise a free kit.
- They mail it to you.
- The kit arrives – it's a "shock and awe" package that includes brochures, piles of testimonials, a catalog of priced inventory, and a DVD. It's a salesperson in an envelope. It has something for everyone and touches upon all of the different buyer personas. The "Researcher" will appreciate this the most.
- They follow up with an email looking for feedback with a deadline on specially timed savings along with a free gift.

It's classic lead-capture 101. This is how you get people to make non-urgent purchases with consistency: you elongate your sales funnel. It's a commonly successful strategy for larger ticket items. On everything from furnace replacement to cosmetic surgery, the trick is to introduce yourself as an expert with a valuable asset, to build trust, capture contact information, and to pursue the lead until the end of the cycle. This is where being positioned as the local authority really comes in handy!

So those are your three main buyer profiles. What's important to realize is that these three prospects exist in every market – the spectrum covered by my simple Buyer's Triangle is practically infinite. You just need to know how to reach them. Communicating effectively with the customers you want is exactly what the next section is going to teach you to do.

4.2 - The 10 Rules of Killer Ad Copy

Alright, now let's get down to the real nitty-gritty. We've talked about the people you're trying to advertise to, and hopefully you've given some thought to who your own ideal customers, clients, and patients are and how to reach them. Now we're really going to get into the science of writing perfect copy for PPC ads, as well as the art form of sales that takes years of practice to master.

Here are the 10 rules that all modern PPC ad copy must abide by before it is truly optimized for attracting leads.

In your market, there are hundreds of thousands of people who could potentially do business with you. However, there is only a handful at one time who are searching for your precise products and services, so you have to be smart and strategic about how you target them. You need strategies you can implement to narrow your market and attract only your very best clients.

This is what you need to know in order to do that:

1. Practice Direct Response Advertising – What is a direct response ad? Basically, direct response ads are advertisements that have a very specific type of "pain" in mind that they address with a solution and a call-to-action.

You've seen them all your life, and you've probably bought from them yourself. The direct response ad formula works because it doesn't waste any time. Plus, it's benefits driven: it knows that there's a challenge, and it offers a solution to the problem. All of your ads should be styled as direct responses to your customer's pain.

All direct response ads have the same basic anatomy:

- **Introduce Pain** – This is the customer's problem, the issue they need to get rid of.

- **Exploit Pain** – Demonstrate all of the ways that pain can impact the potential buyer's life, and how it can get worse if not addressed.

- **Solution** – Your product. Fast-acting, affordable, and efficient.

- **Benefits** – "Here's what life will look like once that pain is taken care of."

- **Urgency** – Revisit pain, introduce deadlines.

- **Limited Availability** – Contribute to urgency with a restricted sales deal or scarcity.

- **Call-to-Action** – Tell your customer exactly what they need to do in order to get your product. The call-to-action should be everywhere: your phone number needs to be visible, and your website needs to be clickable (or at least simple enough to remember). Having an ad with no call-to-action is like showing up to work naked.

This simple and powerful formula works. Properly creating each individual piece takes time, effort, and skill, but the formula is always the same. No matter what stage of your sales funnel you are in – whether you're trying to make people buy the sample package or make the full-on purchase – your ad copy should always be structured in this exact way.

2. Weigh Your Ad Positioning Options – In the immortal words of AC/DC: "*It's a long way to the top if you wanna rock and roll.*" The same can be said for when you want an ad to be the top result.

But you don't always have to reach first position all the time in order to make your ad copy effective. In fact, when targeting some customers, clients, or patients, it's expected that they will pass by the first three or four ads before finding the offer that they want, especially if the pain lacks urgency. So here are some tips to spend half on bids and double your lead conversion by properly managing the position that your ad needs.

The longer the sales cycle and ticket, the less you should be spending on bids. Your competitors are most likely doing the exact opposite – that's because the more intuitive approach is to spend more on the advertising for products that cost more. But this is simply not the best practice when it comes to pay-per-click marketing. Most people researching a larger-scale purchase don't just blindly click the top link – they self-select ads from the right side or middle of the page. Some examples where this has proven to be the case include large ticket items like:

- AC Replacement
- Generator Sales
- Dental Implants
- Exterior Home Improvements

For the scientific thinker in all of us, there are a wide array of research studies available on "PPC heat maps": these visual representations show where a Google user's eyes land first when the results page is brought up. Researchers have also plotted out heat maps of where people are most likely to click. Many of the findings in PPC heat map studies show that being "above the fold" (i.e. visible on the page before scrolling) gives your ad a significant advantage over the links lower down – but that should be obvious.

Where it gets interesting is when you compare the "above the fold" heat maps between different searches. For instance, a search for "best pizza in Chicago" has the highest concentration of "heat" up at the top of the page[38] – but when users searched for something more intensive, like "physical therapy," their eyes tended to concentrate closer to the third link down.[39] Why? Because the former is a "Give It to Me Now" type of search – the user is craving pizza, and they're going to click the first link that catches their eye – and the second is a "Researcher" type. The latter customer doesn't want immediate results so much as they want to find the right fit.

Now that PPC has been around for a little while, experts have been able to compile some historical trends. Recent studies showed that click-through rates of the sponsored ads in the right column have dropped to less than a third of what they were in 2005, and the direction of people's attention has been steadily shifting downwards.[40] A number of conditions could be influencing this, including a preference for organic links – however, the trend could also be the result of ad extensions rising to greater CTR prevalence. This theory is supported by evidence in the "best pizza" article that showed searchers' eyes were drawn towards ad extension features such as site links.

We'll discuss more about ad extensions further down the line. Right now, we'll stick to the basics, like answering the phone.

3. It Pays To Be the First Guy to Pick Up the Phone – When you do want to be at the very top result (i.e. when you're looking for the "Give It to Me Now" lead who is probably googling your product or service on his smartphone), try to think of it as if it's the yellow pages. Remember the yellow pages? Whenever you needed a solution fast, you'd go to the phone book and start searching through the service providers. You'd call one guy, and if he didn't pick up the first time, you call the next guy.

In the event of demand-driven service, my experience has been that most people treat paid ads as if they are flipping through the phone book. For certain services that have a high degree of urgency, the #1 position is key.

And you have to be prepared for it by answering your phone.

Demand-driven businesses will always get a much higher conversion rate compared to product-driven campaigns. Your sales funnel needs to be longer for larger ticket items. But for those "Give It to Me Now" calls, it is critical to be ready for the drop.

4. Google AdWords is in Real-Time, Baby! – Have you ever watched *Mad Men*? You already know my favorite quote from it, at least. *Mad Men* is a show about the 5th Avenue ad agencies from the 50s and 60s. That was an era of serious money being in ad copy. It was a fast-paced world, to be sure – but that was nothing compared to advertising now.

Shows like *Mad Men* make you realize that these ad copy rules are nothing new. In fact, the principles I'm laying out for you about direct response ads were mostly developed in the early 20th century by a man named Claude Hopkins. Today, some people know Hopkins as the man who made toothpaste a household item through his marketing. He also developed a list of ad copy best practices in his book, *Scientific Advertising.*

Marketing experts have been using these practices for almost a century now.

But you have to remember that, back then, those guys were writing stuff for billboards, basic cable commercials, and radio ads. They were using direct mail, newspapers, and magazines – mediums that would take time to get to the front porch. It took days, weeks, and even months to determine whether ad copy was working or not. As sharp as Don Draper may be, he still has to wait 30 days or so, sometimes more, to see if the copy he wrote is converting the way he wants.

The waiting period is what the show *Mad Men* cuts out.

Imagine if those guys had been able to know in just a few hours if the copy they wrote was converting. Imagine if they could send out an ad, see if it's performing the way they want, then take it back and try writing the sales copy a different way to improve conversion results – all over the course of a single day. Imagine if they could split-test two ads at once on a Monday and have the answer of which one was outperforming the other by that Friday. What would happen?

They'd be unstoppable, that's what!

Well, believe it or not, all of those hypotheticals I just mentioned are the reality of what Google AdWords allows you to do.

AdWords ads appear almost immediately, since they move at the speed of the internet. Besides the brief configuration and evaluation period your ads experience when they're turned on for the first time, there's very little waiting to do at all. If you notice you're not getting impressions within a few days, there's something wrong – you need to change it up.

So you do! Google AdWords operates in real-time, so ads can be corrected, stopped, and ramped up over the course of the day, week, or month. Once you have ad copy in your PPC campaign that you know works, you can use that top-performing sales piece for your direct mailings and in your email subject lines as well – using AdWords ad copy that is proven to work will improve your conversion in other channels.

Pay-per-click advertising is Don Draper's dream come true, and you're living it right now. How well do your current campaigns take advantage of that?

5. Be Relevant by Timing Your Ads Throughout the Day – Part of the fact that Google AdWords PPC occurs in real-time means that you can customize your ads based on the day of the week, or even the time of day. Have you noticed that more calls come in on Mondays? Then you can adjust your PPC budget to make higher and more frequent bids at the start of the week. Do your emergency calls tend to come in around midnight? You can run certain ads during the wee hours to capture those "Give It to Me Now" leads.

Here are some examples:

- **Same Day Plumbing Service** – The plumber who books same day service when you call before 11am will run that ad between 6am and 11am – which is when most people notice they have a drain clog in their toilet or shower.

- **Dentist On Call** – The ad copy for a dentist who performs on nights and weekends might say "Call 24/7 for a Live Dentist to get Emergency Dental Care." If you run those ads late at night and on Saturdays and Sundays, you'll have the customers who chip their teeth or have extreme pains finding and clicking on your ads first.

- **The "Better Call Saul" Style Attorney** – In the show *Breaking Bad*, one of the characters is a lawyer who deals with emergency-level cases. But you don't have to be Saul to know your ads for DUI defense are going to be more effective when they run in the evening on Friday and Saturday nights.

Google AdWords gives you the ability to reach the audience you want based on when your calls come in – you can up your strategy to the next level entirely just by promising to return calls at certain times. Again: is your current strategy seizing these opportunities?

6. Be Aware of the Current Events that Impact Your Buyers' Lives – As a small business owner, you should always know what's going on in your market. Conditions that might change the way your customers are living should also change the way that you advertise. Google AdWords helps you be hyper-relevant to local problems or environmental conditions that impact your ideal customers, clients, or patients.

One of the best examples of event impact is extreme weather. Heavy rains mean that waterproofing companies need to up their AdWords budget and increase their high-demand presence: nothing makes people want to call for sump pump installation quite like a flooded basement. Real-time budget control helps you seize whatever opportunities the weather brings.

But even more so than your bid strategy, your ad copy should change to account for local events. For instance, generator sales companies who run ads with the names of contemporary hurricanes tend to receive more calls – mainly because they double up on visibility, since now the people looking for storm updates will also notice their company and tie it back to the name of the hurricane. Similarly, generator installers might aggressively market to one neighborhood or city in particular during a power outage. Tree removal services can do the same thing.

And don't think taking advantage of weather conditions is just for service contractors. Consider, for example, a personal injury attorney: when conditions are icy and slick, demand tends to go up. There are also regular calendar events that should impact the way you advertise year over year – for instance, gym owners know how to customize their sales copy for holidays and New Year's Resolutions. The bottom line is that it pays to stay up to date.

7. Be Unique and Don't Just do What Your Market Does – Following a formulaic approach has its place in advertising: in fact, you should still follow the structure of direct response advertising (Ad Copy Rule #1) regardless of what the rest of your market is doing. Direct response advertising is a strategy that doesn't change.

But at the same time, you have to distinguish yourself. Within the structure of a direct response ad, there are many opportunities to stand out. I'm advocating that you do the complete reverse of what your competition is doing. When you notice the trend of a local market going in one direction, then it's time to go the opposite way. All of your competitors will be copying each other and not covering any real ground, whereas you will be blazing a trail.

When there's no driving force in a market to go against the current, you tend to get static patterns in AdWords sales copy. Standard-style ads can go lame because companies aren't differentiating themselves. As a result, price-driven markets fail to capitalize on demand. For instance, take a look at the drain cleaning market in Los Angeles. When you go to Google and type in "Los Angeles drain cleaning," this is what you get:

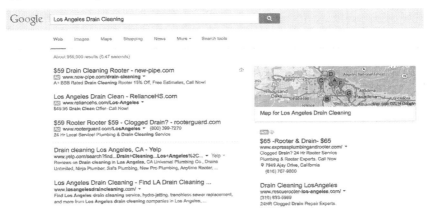

What stands out to you here?

That's right: *nothing much.*

My point is that everyone is running essentially the same ad. Somewhere between the $30 dollar and $65 drain cleaning, there's competition. But none of the competitors are competing the right way! Not a single ad mentions immediate response. Everyone sees that the next guy is running a cheap drain cleaning offer, so they try to run a cheaper one. That's no way to drive up revenue, and it's no way to run efficient PPC.

This is where advertising transitions from being a science to being an art. Crafting ad copy that stands out is a creative process, and it requires thought, planning, and a little imagination. How can you stand out in your field? What can you do differently?

Here's how I would play the LA drain cleaning market. First, you need to realize that drain cleaning is an urgent service, not a product. People who have seriously clogged toilets or showers aren't looking to save a buck – they're looking for someone who can fix their problem today so that they can get back on track with their lives. So instead of making my ad copy about how much you can save, I'd make it about *how quick we can get there*. "Same Day Service: we'll be there within an hour of your call." This method works because:

- It appeals to what the customer needs, not to what the market trend is doing.

- It makes you visible, instead of being one drop in a sea of "Dollars Off."

- It automatically disqualifies the budget conscious buyer persona who does not have an urgent problem. You do not need price-sensitive buyers hassling you for deals on a $50-100 job.

Getting your ads in the top results for your keywords is just the first step. From there, successful advertising becomes all about being more visible than the other guy. I know how to get to the top for the keywords that matter, and I know how to stand out once I'm there. I've made drain cleaning campaigns consistently successful by finding the current movement of the local market and *going in the exact opposite direction.*

8. Optimize Your Landing Pages with Matching Copy – Landing pages play perhaps the most critical role in lead conversion out of any part of your campaigns. 50% of Google AdWords success happens on your landing page. The page that your ad takes clients to is a critical lead-conversion component for any campaign. Your ad copy, then, needs to make a strong enough statement that your landing page can expound upon it.

If you dissect an optimized landing page, you'll wind up with more or less the same parts as were described in the direct response ad. Crafting a landing page tends to be more complicated than writing PPC ad copy since there's far more room to work with, but the basic principles – pain, exploit pain, solution, benefits, call-to-action – are all the same. We'll discuss this in more detail in the next chapter.

First and foremost, though, you need to make sure your landing pages follow this basic rule: the message of your landing page needs to always match the message of your ad copy. No exceptions! This is the only route to optimal conversion.

Why is matching the ad copy and the landing page such a high priority? For a couple of reasons: first of all, it's common sense. If you get a prospective customer, client, or patient excited enough to click on your ad, you need to follow up on your offer in more detail. You can't just switch the message, because then they'll just turn around. Second of all, a landing page that contains core keywords improves your overall Google Quality Score.

See, it's pivotal to always remember that Google isn't just looking to please advertisers. Their other customers are their search users – the people who have made Google the most popular search engine in the world. That's why Google doesn't just let you draw customers in with whatever ad copy you want to use. There are rules to the game. If a Google user clicks the top link in the search results and is brought to a completely separate page, that is considered spam.

And Google doesn't tolerate spam.

So that's why Google Quality Scores exist. We first saw this concept back in the "Google AdWords Lexicon," so flip back if you don't remember. When a site's Quality Score is good, the site owner pays less for ad bids, making it easier for them to reach the top where users will find them for relevant keyword searches. That's Google's way of rewarding solid content. When a site's Quality Score is poor, those ads get knocked all the way down, and the user will wind up paying outrageous sums of money for positioning that doesn't convert well. That's the price you pay when you don't use matching landing pages: higher prices and fewer leads.

When properly optimized, landing pages can be a campaign's greatest asset. They will increase your lead conversion, and you can use call-tracking and dynamic swap technology to track that conversion on each individual page! Optimized landing pages are just as important, if not more important, than your Google AdWords setup itself. Your PPC manager needs to have the ability to create landing pages with your branding, and they need to be made the right way.

So when monitoring your landing pages, keep an eye out for the following negative trend: high click-through rate (CTR), low conversion. That means you have lots of people clicking on your ad and winding up on the landing page, but very few people deciding they want to call. This progression is a sign that there is something wrong with the way your landing page is interacting with your ad copy to direct prospects. Does your landing page follow the structure of a direct response ad? Is the wording confusing? Does it have a clear, concise call-to-action? *Does it accurately match the statements being made in the ad?* You know that your ads are getting people to click, but you need to fix that landing page so that it makes people act. Landing page optimization is what I'm going to cover in depth in the next chapter.

A good PPC manager will identify the high CTR/low conversion trend quickly and take corrective action by split-testing landing pages on the ads that are performing well – namely, the ones that have the highest CTR. Which brings me to the next rule:

9. Always Split-Test Ads with Minor Variations – What's the difference between an ad that says "Same Day Service" and another that says "Get Service Same Day?" Nothing, in terms of what's being offered. But it could be a difference maker in the amount of leads you generate.

That's why split-testing ad copy is so important. We might not always realize it, but our minds can be very picky about the way ads are worded! A simple modification of sentence structure could make the difference between an ad with 1 click and an ad with 100 clicks.

I'm always saying that you need to follow proven strategies and optimize your marketing time-investment, so how can I also say that you need to experiment with ad copy and make decisions based on trial and error?

The reason is because split-testing actually helps you get *more* out of your budget, even if the first couple of ads you run don't convert at all. How? Let's do some quick back-of-the-napkin math. In this scenario, you're a dentist looking to sell professional teeth whitening. You run an offer for "$100 Off Professional Teeth Whitening" in the ad copy.

- Say you spend **$1000** a month on a specific campaign.
- That $1000 buys you **10,000** impressions and a **1%** click-

through rate, which yields 100 clicks.

- You drive people to an optimized landing page that converts **25%** of clicks into leads, meaning you now have **25 leads**. (100 clicks at 25% conversion)

Not too bad…but what if it could be better? You could work on your landing pages and probably improve conversion by 5 points, and I recommend you do that – it means you'll generate 5 more leads. However, the weakest link in this scenario is your click-through rate. You have plenty of traffic but you're not getting as many clicks on your ads as you could. If you got 1% of 10,000 people to take action, that means 9,900 people searched for your service, saw your ad, and went somewhere else instead. It happens – but by split-testing another ad at the same time, you might be able to get a slightly better click-through rate on the same campaign. Split-testing is the ongoing process of whittling down our ad copy – think of it as *sharpening our hunting spear.*

So you split-test your ad copy and put it up against a competing offer, and you notice that the ad you run saying "$299 Professional Teeth Whitening" has a 2% click-through rate compared to the 1% CTR of the "$100 Off" copy. It's just a slight difference, right? Well a 1% improvement on CTR can double your lead volume if everything else stays the same. Could that 1% improvement be worth the time that you spent running two separate ads at once under the same budget? You betcha!

Here's what the math looks like when we improve our CTR by only 1%:

- You get the same **10,000** impressions, but now at a **2%** CTR.
- This results in **200 clicks**.
- The landing page is still optimized, so it converts at **25%**.
- Now you wind up with **50 leads**, and you're free to continue the process.

Yes, conversion is still king, but even the tiniest upgrade on your CTR can make a dramatic difference when applied in conjunction with a solid landing page! The slight increase of 1% just doubled our lead volume. So is split-testing ad copy worth the time and effort of the experimentation?

Absolutely.

10. Use Ad Extensions to Enhance Conversion – The final rule for making killer ad copy for your Google AdWords campaigns is simple: know your ad extensions and how to use them.

What are ad extensions? According to Google, this is the definition:

○ **Ad extensions** – a type of ad format that shows extra information ("extending" from your text ads) about your business. Some can be added manually and others are automated.

In more basic terms, ad extensions are additional items you can include in your ads to help them convert at a much higher level. They show up alongside your ad links and allow your prospects to do different things besides just click. Some extensions are automated, so they come up as part of all PPC ad copy: these include features such as "consumer ratings," "previous visitations," "seller ratings," "dynamic sitelink extensions," and "social extensions," all of which are visible to your potential customers by default. But the ones I want to focus on are the extensions you need to *manually turn on*, without which your ad copy may be incomplete.

Here are the manual extensions currently available. Are you using the ones you need yet?

- **Call Extension** – I've referred to the importance of mobile search several times– this is just one of many instances where it comes into play. Using the call extension on your ads creates a little phone symbol next to your number that allows mobile users to call you directly by clicking.

    EXAMPLE: Let's say you run a taxi service. You know that people are looking for you on their smartphones, and when they see your ads they want to be connected to you in the quickest way possible. You need the call extension button in order to snag that last-minute lead. Without it, your demand-driven ads aren't optimized properly.

- **Location Extension** – Don't make your customers go searching for you in all different places – the majority of them won't bother. Using the location extension creates a clickable address below your ad so that prospective customers can automatically receive directions to your store. Have you ever used your smartphone as a GPS and had to Google search directions while driving? I won't comment any further, other than to say that you could really save a life with this one.

EXAMPLE: Restaurant owners need location apps so that people can find their storefront when they're looking for food on the move. When somebody's craving Italian, they aren't going to spend ten minutes trying to find your location so they can copy and paste it into their GPS app. Be smart and give the people what they want.

- **Review Extension** – This is useful for any and all service providers, so heads up! The review extension adds a line of text beneath your ad copy link with a brief rating or testimonial. It might say "Rated #1 in CITY" or have a brief quote from a third party.

  EXAMPLE: Prospective customers to plumbing contractors frequently want to see reviews before they buy in order to make sure the company they're dealing with isn't known for ripping people off. Put those reviews right where they can see them!

- **Download Extension** – The fourth extension app we'll cover is fairly straightforward. The download extension creates a button next to your ad that allows people to immediately download the sample or PDF you are offering.

  EXAMPLE: You're a programming company that has built a media playing software that you want people to buy, but first you need them to try out the demo. The download extension allows your prospective customers to download the demo version on any device so they enter your sales funnel without even having to go to your landing page.

- **App Extension** – It's possible that your business doesn't have an app – the process to make one can be rather costly, not to mention involved. However, having an app (i.e. a small program that resides on a portable device, such as a cell phone) offers several potential advantages, including brand immersion and more effective mobile marketing. If you are a company that has or needs an app, then you also need the app extension on Google AdWords, which takes the user to a virtual store where they can buy or download your program straight away.

EXAMPLE: Have you ever tried to use Yelp on your phone? It can be clumsy and frustrating to type into small and slow-loading searchbars on your phone's mobile internet or public Wi-Fi. That's why Yelp has an app extension to always give on-the-go users a simple way of searching. Plus, the app (necessarily) requires the customer's location, which helps them to target-advertise more specifically.

- **Site Link Extension** – Have you ever searched for a site and noticed that the ad has several blue links below or beside the main page title? Those are site links, and they increase user-mobility. Using site links, searchers can navigate directly to the section of your site they need to see, rather than having to go to the homepage and then redirect themselves from there. Improving your site visitors' experience always results in more leads.

  EXAMPLE: You're a vascular surgeon offering several separate treatments for artery and vein diseases that you want customers to be aware of when they reach your advertisements. One sitelink can be for endovascular therapy, another can be for angioplasty, another for surgical blood clot removal, and each will bring your clients to a related page your website for more information.

  Callout Extension – These are additions to your ad copy that draw focus to specific features of your service. They generally appear directly below the main link.

  EXAMPLE: An electronics company that ships products for free and has customer service representatives working round the clock will want to place "Free Shipping" and "24-Hour Customer Service" callouts in their PPC ads.

Google warns you that ad extensions don't always show up, but they don't have any extra cost apart from the usual CPC, so you'd be silly not to have them working for you when they are relevant. After all, the Google AdWords game is all about making optimal use of every tool at your disposal.

Creating highly converting ad copy is both an art and a science. It takes years of practice and ongoing testing to get truly good at it – and even then, there's still more to learn.

BONUS RESOURCES FOR "HUNTING YOUR FOOD"

Get Steve's Ad Copy Survival Blueprint ($97 value): This is the actual tool Steve uses with clients to develop a go-to market strategy for each and every campaign he manages. This tool will make sure you don't miss a thing when you begin to craft your ad copy for Google AdWords.

Get Steve's Ad Copy Tool ($97 value): This simple and powerful one page worksheet gives you the ability to simulate and test your ad copy. It will tell you exactly how many characters you can fit into your ad. In addition, it will show you an example of how it will appear on Google's search results page.

Plus Receive: A complimentary One-on-One 20-Minute ad copy review with an experienced PPC lead generation and conversion specialist that works directly for Steve.

Join Pay-Per-Click Prosperity – the place for better Google AdWords performance – and access all of these resources today.
Go to: payperclickprosperity.com

Chapter 4 Survivor's Summary

The two sub-sections of this chapter were "Knowing Your Ideal Customer" and the "The 10 Rules of Killer Ad Copy." The former introduced us to the "Buyer's Triangle" and the three separate buyer personas while the latter showed us ten proven strategies to improve CTR and lead generation.

In order to know our ideal customer, we first needed to talk about understanding the prospect's pain. Every buyer can be qualified by their level of demand, their price range, and their willingness to research. This gives us a sense of how to distinguish the 3 main types of buyers and how to appeal to each.

Learning how to craft killer ad copy started with dissecting the structure of a direct response ad. From there, we moved into discussing the rules of ad positioning, ad timing, copy optimization, and the use of ad extensions.

Your takeaways from this chapter should be how to target ads, what the direct response format is, and how to write sales copy that converts.

Test Your Survival Skills: *(Find answers on page 190)*

1. A Google user looking to buy Invisalign fittings might be an example of the _____ buyer persona, especially if they take the time to search for testimonials, read FAQs, and download "Before and After" photos.

2. Money-back guarantees and Price-Match policies are examples of _____, which can help you advertise to "Value-Driven" shoppers.

3. The main reason that making your landing page match the ad copy is so important is because otherwise your _____ will suffer.

4. When you Google search for "Chinese food in Somerville" on your smartphone and the first result has a clickable phone number to their delivery line, that's a wise use of the _____, a feature available on AdWords.

5 | Finding Water

The 5 Landing Page Mistakes Your PPC Manager is Making and How to Fix Them

5.1 - What Are Landing Pages?

So you've got your technology and you've got your ad copy. You've accounted for your shelter and your food, which is a great start. All of the tools are at your disposal to create a stable PPC campaign with high conversion...except for one thing.

You need to optimize your landing pages.

In my experience, landing page optimization is the most common difference between AdWords success and total marketing failure. While your technology protects you and your ad copy sustains you, landing pages are what give your campaigns life. That's why optimized landing pages for an AdWords user can be compared to the 3rd and most important survival necessity: water.

In this chapter, you'll discover how to make landing pages that convert at high rates. You'll see common failures contrasted with best practices. Remember, the distinction between a low-converting landing page and an optimized one is like the difference between the ocean and drinkable water: the first is of no use to you – the other will keep you alive.

Of course, landing page optimization starts with knowing exactly what a landing page is, so here's a basic definition:

- **Dedicated PPC Landing Page** – the webpage that your potential customers reach by clicking on one of your pay-per-click ads. It contains further information about the direct offer your ad is making and advises the viewer on how to proceed. It is designed to collect information and to advance the prospect to the next stage in the sales process.

Complete landing page optimization is achieved when your landing pages consistently convert quality leads at rates higher than your competitors' campaigns – essentially meaning you get the maximum bang for your Adwords buck.

You need a landing page that the customer will find inviting and engaging. Its purpose is to convince the customer to read the content, trust your company, and ultimately follow the call-to-action. It needs a means of collecting visitor's contact information – for many campaigns, collecting the client's email and phone number will be the first stage of your sales funnel. Most importantly, your landing pages need to be optimized *every step of the way* between a prospect's cursory research and the call that makes the sale. If you aren't properly optimizing your landing pages, then you're losing leads through the cracks.

Unfortunately, this is the case for far too many small businesses. They have PPC managers who make the sales copy, manage their bids, and control the bare essentials of their campaigns – but once people click, they consider their job to be done. Potential customers could be clicking your ads and then *turning right back around* without calling, giving you a high CTR, a depleted budget, and no conversion. I've seen it many times before: in fact, it's one of the first warning signs I look for in a new account.

You see, there are two types of pay-per-click managers. First, you have those who are extremely technical with AdWords, and they essentially just go through the motions of building a functional campaign. Then you have those who offer a *complete solution* including technical aptitude, direct response advertising, and a conversion-driven philosophy. My company offers the complete solutions, because having follow-through from click to ROI is critical to your success.

But before we talk about how to make your own pages the powerful, life-giving resource that can make your campaigns a success, we'll outline how *not* to write a landing page. Make sure your current pages aren't losing traction from these common oversights. The following landing page mistakes cost users thousands of potential ROI every month. If their PPC manager isn't watching closely, they might not even realize that poorly designed landing pages are why the phones aren't ringing.

The 5 Most Common Landing Page Mistakes

If your last PPC campaign committed any of the following blunders, I can tell you with complete confidence that it did not generate as many leads as it could have. Even if your click-through rate was through the roof, these errors caused you to waste precious ad dollars and leave money on the table:

1. **Not Using Dedicated Landing Pages** – I'm always surprised by how many cases I've seen where a prospect will click on a specific ad only to be brought directly to the company's main website home page. The whole point of PPC is to make your message visible and directly engaging to the user. How do you expect to do that if your AdWords clicks don't arrive at a page that makes your promotions apparent? Your potential customers aren't just going to find your offers on their own. A campaign without dedicated landing pages is hardly worth running at all.

2. **Landing Pages Don't Connect to The Website** – Every landing page that you create, whether you base it on your actual site or through an independent design application, ought to give visitors the ability to navigate to your homepage. One effective way to do this is to have your logo (which belongs at the top of every landing page you create) link back to your main site. This ensures that users who want to learn more about your company won't become frustrated when they can't find your primary URL.

   I can't stress enough how important it is that your landing pages present a welcoming and high-quality user experience. If your dedicated landing pages don't swiftly and intuitively link to your main site, you may lose prospective clients.

However, you should know this rule is not 100% definitive. I run campaigns all the time with dedicated vanity URLs – these are landing pages that lock prospects into a squeeze page with long sales copy. For the purposes of a local company, you'll want to test different landing page formats as they relate to conversion. We'll delve further into this later in the chapter.

3. **Page is Not Relevant to Search Words** – Having a landing page that doesn't actually address the topic chosen in your keywords will make you lose ground with Google's Quality Score. In the last chapter, I talked about the importance of maintaining site Quality Score for managing the cost of your AdWords bids. It really is critical that your keywords are appropriately matched with your campaigns, otherwise users and search engines alike are liable to view your landing pages as spam.

4. **Trying to Do Too Much** – Sure, you should always be ambitious with your PPC, but if your campaigns aren't focused then they aren't going to draw in the people you need. The last chapter was all about knowing your audience and how to reach them – well, here is another instance where that knowledge comes into play. Your landing page should be geared towards the type of customer that you're looking to bring in as a lead, and *only* that one type. Remember our customer profiles: which of the buyers is your campaign addressing, and how does your landing page appeal to that visitor?

    EXAMPLE: Let's use a scenario where you're looking to attract the attention of someone early in their decision-making process – say you're selling a dental implant procedure for $15,000. Now you need a "first-step" style landing page to catch the visitor in your sales funnel. This prospect doesn't know about you yet, but he's interested in purchasing dental implants and is looking for the most affordable route. What should the direct offer of your landing page be: a free report, or an initial consultation? A free report could include a collection of before-and-after photographs to demonstrate exactly what the procedure does. An initial consultation, on the other hand, would involve the patient actually coming to the office and receiving a cost evaluation of the implants.

Both are good pages to test – however, you will create more leads if you offer the free report. By creating a dental implants landing page that offers a FREE "Before and After" picture report, you'll convert more prospects who are early in the buying process – namely "Researchers" who are looking for informative material. Plus, delivering an asset is a valuable opportunity to start nurturing and qualifying leads.

As a savvy marketer, you can also work in typical objections you'd face in the buying process to your report. For example, if you know you lose 40% of your opportunities due to budgeting, then you can talk about financing options.

Figuring out how to market your landing pages to specific customer profiles takes practice. The process is similar to crafting ad copy, but landing pages need to be much more substantial – there's more space to work with, and it needs to be filled in correctly. There's a lot of psychology that goes into it. What percentage of your content is going to be informative? What percentage will be sales-based? Make sure whoever is creating your landing pages has the experience and skill that it takes to specifically profile and target your leads for each individual campaign you run, otherwise you'll be losing money.

5. **Failing to Build Credibility** – Does your landing page tell potential customers why they should trust your company and not go to someone else? Every landing page you make should tie in to your branding and reputation. Make sure that your landing page establishes you as the resident expert in your field. If your dedicated landing pages do not include at least a turnkey set of differentiators as a persuasion tool, you're not including the complete functionality that those pages should have.

These are the five ways not to create successful landing pages. All too often, small businesses lose out because their PPC manager is making one or several of these amateur mistakes. To be a winner in Google AdWords, you'll need to stay clear of these pitfalls.

Now that we've covered how *not* to write landing pages, let's find out how an AdWords user constructs a winning landing page for their PPC campaign. The next two sections will guide us through the fundamental preparations that make landing pages convert at the level that they should.

5.2 - The Basics of Landing Pages

While the AdWords management "sinkers" are getting caught in the low-conversion traps I described above, the AdWords "swimmer" is applying these simple best practices to get his sales funnel operating at full capacity:

1. **Landing Pages are "Naked"** – When I say "naked," I mean that they don't have links to any other pages (apart from the link to your main website embedded in the logo). A quality landing page should feel like the end goal for the customer, client, or patient. They should arrive there and think, "This is exactly where I want to be." So, to that end, there should be no other routes that a customer feels they need to take other than the call-to-action. They should either:

   A. Reach the landing page and order your product/service immediately.

   B. Fill out the form on the landing page that takes them to the next step in your sales funnel.

   Don't clutter your landing pages unnecessarily – make sure that each one is completely without any other necessary online navigation paths. Keep it clean and simple. Remember, the goal is conversion.

2. **Must Include Your Keyword** – This should be straightforward enough. Whenever you create an ad with a dedicated landing page, you need it to contain the keywords you're bidding for. Having multiple mentions and variations of your keyword in your landing page is the best practice for ensuring clarity and site quality. To ensure optimization, my company will create a landing page for every single adgroup we manage – this makes your campaign more comprehensive.

3. **A Clear-Cut Call-to-Action** – Speaking of clarity, here is the stage where crystal clear communication becomes immensely important. Our definition of dedicated landing pages mentioned that they should specifically instruct potential clients how to proceed. This step is known as a "call-to action."

   EXAMPLES:

   - "Call 888-CONNECT Today"
   - "Fill Out the Form for a FREE E-Book"
   - "Enter Your Address to Receive a Sample Kit"
   - "Request Consultation Here"
   - "Download Your FREE Report"

   Your call-to-action should be concise, direct, and reiterated several times throughout the page. Ideally, your landing page should have just one call-to-action, and that directive should appear above the phone number, in the form, at the foot of the page, and in the body of the content. That way, customers who reach the page know exactly what to do next.

4. **Limit Contact Options** – To follow up on the point I just made: your landing page shouldn't have a whole host of call-to-action options. By "options," I mean different channels through which they can complete the purchase or step. There are dozens of means for a customer to get in touch with you – these include communicating via email, on live chat, over the phone, and through a lead-capture form. However, you don't want to introduce them all at once. Giving the reader too many options to choose from can be overwhelming – and besides, if you offer them all at once, you won't know which one is the most effective. Limit your contact methods to a maximum of two. For same day service opportunities, I prefer to push people towards making the phone call: it's the most straightforward approach, and the response is immediate. Lead capture forms are my personal first choice when I'm looking to add info to a listserv. If you're testing out a landing page, live chat can be a useful tool as well: through instant messaging back-and-forth with page viewers, you can record what the most frequently

asked questions are and incorporate the answers into your sales copy.

5. **Optimized for Mobile Devices** – The homeowner standing in a flooded basement doesn't want to log onto his computer to find a water heater replacement deal. Mobile search is becoming infinitely more convenient with each passing year, and as a result, its rate has been skyrocketing. Back in the "Technology" chapter, I gave you some statistics to show the growth of mobile search, which included Google's estimation that mobile would be overtaking desktop search in 2015. It's also worth noting the rapidly growing number of alternative devices that are in use across the U.S. – here are some additional stats:

More Statistics of Mobile Search[41]

- 80% of respondents to the 2014 Mobile Behavior Report agreed that mobile devices are a central part of their everyday lives.

- 73% of smartphone owners also own a tablet.

- 81% of people in the $75-100K earnings bracket own tablets.

- 54% of mobile users say it's easier for them to find info on mobile websites, but more than half said mobile sites typically don't supply enough information.

In other words, mobile users prioritize a seamless content viewing experience between all of their devices, but more than half are still unsatisfied. I've said it before and I'll say it again: give the people what they want. Make sure your landing pages are optimized for mobile viewing on both smartphones and tablets, and that mobile pages present informative, clear content.

6. **Be Informative and Build Trust** – Failing to build credibility was one of the 5 most common landing page mistakes I discussed in the last section. Now I'm going to show you how to fix lackluster differentiators and position yourself as an authority.

Every landing page you write needs to answer the following questions:

A. What is my company going to do for the customer, client, or patient that nobody else is doing?

B. What information do I bring to the table that proves I'm an "expert?"

C. What are my customers, clients, or patients saying about my company?

How is credibility "built?" What tools do you use to answer the questions above? Here are the three best trust-building tactics:

- **Testimonials** – The best and most straightforward way to establish your legitimacy as a company is to prominently include testimonials on your landing pages. But how do you get testimonials from your customers?

  Simple: just ask.

  You'd be shocked by how willing people are to talk about their experience if you do a good job. Ask for just a moment of their time to leave a comment on one of your social media sites – or even ask them if they'd be interested in appearing in a brief video. Some might decline, but all you need is a few to say "yes."

  Do you currently have a review page linked out from your website? Do you encourage customers to review your service on social media outlets? If you don't, you're missing out on a valuable opportunity. By requesting comments and reviews that can later be used as landing page testimonials, you capitalize on your best credibility resource: customer satisfaction. Have you ever been asked to participate in a survey after you got off the phone with, say, your insurance provider? That's so they can use that review later in their marketing efforts. Testimonials are critical for your ads.

- **Differentiators** – Any landing page you make should include clear, concise reasons why people should buy from you instead of your competitors. What sets you apart? What do you offer that no one else does? These qualities are called differentiators, and they should be a part of every landing page you make.

  EXAMPLE: "We are the only residential energy company that

offers financing on all of our product models and full warranties for every installation."

- **Informative Guide** – Ask yourself: what do you think your ideal customer immediately wants to know when considering a purchase from your company? When you're making a dedicated landing page, preempt the answer to that question.

  For instance, if you think that your customers want to know the approximate costs of what they're getting (typical for large ticket items), provide a buyer's guide that includes price estimations – or even offer over-the-phone quotes. This is a smart strategy to disqualify time-wasters. If you think that your customers want to know how your product works, include diagrams and infographics that explain. Put together an FAQ web page or downloadable sheet! The point here is to predict and solve the customer's biggest hang-ups so they will continue to rely on you as an advisor.

7. **Solid Code Base** – Test your landing pages to make sure they work on all the major browsers including Mozilla, Chrome, Safari, and Explorer. This one check will save you the pain of discovering later on down that line that some of your prospects are having problems viewing your offers.

8. **Install Good Copy** – When you're working with Google AdWords, the sales copy doesn't end at the click. Your landing page should also be structured as direct response ads: that means they follow the same structure from before:

   A. Describe Pain

   B. Exploit Pain

   C. Introduce Solution

   D. List Benefits

   E. Call-to-Action

   You'd be surprised by how many folks allow other, less important matters to interfere with the proven formula. The flow of their landing pages gets interrupted by irrelevant, weak, or otherwise not necessary *fluff*, and as a result their clicks don't convert.

Which brings me to my next point: even though these are the landing page "basics," the finished product really doesn't need to be that much more complicated. In fact, when it comes to conversion, simpler is better. *You don't need to bring the circus.* Flashy fonts, animated GIFs, and interactive videos are all very cool, but they ultimately hurt your conversion in the likely event that they fail to load correctly or that they distract from the message of the copy. The page should get straight to the point in an easily readable and modestly branded style.

5.3 - Landing Page Sales Copy Structure

I mentioned the direct response format above, and I'm always going to stress simplicity in landing page structure. First and foremost, eliminate the waste and follow the basics.

However, when it comes to making a direct response template that *specifically fits your call-to-action,* you may need some more in-depth instruction. I've broken down the landing page copy structure into two distinct formats to help you get started.

Format 1 – The Pain Dynamic

This format is for a situation where your prospective customer is in tangible pain. They're worried, they're struggling, and they're looking for someone who understands. This is the more direct of the two structures, and as a result it's relatively short – it typically speaks best to "Give It to Me Now" persona customers. I'll use an example to clarify: in this instance, imagine you're a social security disability advocate. You deal with collecting social security benefits for people who can't work. Here's how one of your landing pages might look:

1. **Identify the Problem** – "Are you out of work due to an injury? Now you need your disability benefits – and fast. But you're so overwhelmed by the process of applying for Social Security that you don't even know where to start."

2. **Agitate the Problem** – "The government has made this a

huge hassle, and you've got bills that need to be paid. You're a hardworking person, and you've contributed for years, but you've fallen on hard times: you can't risk having your application turned down by the SSA. You need someone to be on your side in this fight."

3. **Offer the Solution** – "We're the Social Security experts, and we're here to help. Work with us, because we don't charge a dime until we get the disability money you deserve."

Simple and straight to the point. The key is to start with the basic pain and then talk about how that pain can escalate as time progresses. Throw gas on the fire: emphasize the issue until it's a full-blown disaster, and then tell them what you can do to fix it.

The Pain Dynamic format isn't only good for urgent situations, though. It can be easily used in long-term sales cycles – you just need to know how to drum up urgency with a *what-could-go-wrong* scenario.

Format 2 – Challenge Assignment

In this template, the "pain" is replaced with a challenge. Rather than addressing a problem with a solution, this landing page presents a resource or amenity for the buyer's consideration. The sales funnel on this type of landing page tends to be longer and more informative, and the target audience is generally more along the lines of a "Value-Driven" or "Researcher" profile – however, just like with the Pain Dynamic, there is the opportunity to have reliable ad copy success with this format in any scenario if you *know your ideal customer well.*

Either way, though, the structure goes as follows. You've definitely seen commercials that follow this style. For this format, we'll use a product example, specifically a landing page advertising the sale of surround-sound speakers.

1. **Introduce Challenge/Goal** – "What if you could enjoy every movie night like you're in the theater? Or listen to music and feel like you're at a live concert?"

2. **Expand Upon Challenge/Goal** – "Discover a new entertainment experience with the audio system that your home deserves."

3. **Tease the Solution** – "Now you can get cinema-quality sound for an all-time low price. The next level of entertainment is on the horizon."

4. **Soft-Close With a Call-to-Action** – "Call today, and you can get our premium AudioAddict™ system for just $729."

5. **List Benefits of Solution** – "Surround sound lets you watch movies, play games, and listen to music like never before. Get the full experience that your TV has to offer."

6. **Testimonials or Reviews** – "Movie director Michael Bay gives our equipment 5 stars: 'It's the only way to watch *Transformers 7.*'"

7. **Restate the Solution** – "The AudioAddict™ sets the industry standard for crisp, beautiful audio with any television system."

8. **Features of Service/Product** – "Each speaker comes with adjustable volume control for pitch-perfect sound regulation."

9. **More Testimonials** – "Ken Dashow of Q104.3 says, 'It's not just good sound, it's the best sound. You've never heard anything like it.'"

10. **Restate Solution and Call-to-Action** – "Our experts will install AudioAddict™ in the perfect style to complete your home's entertainment system today. Call 1-800-MY-SOUND today for details."

Sound sort of familiar? That's because this is the structure of just about any infomercial you see on television. It works in landing page format too! And you don't have to have product praise from Michael Bay to make it work – all it takes is some decent customer reviews and some creatively worded copy. These two formats have everything you need to make any campaign convert.

5.4 - The Types of Landing Pages

Now that you know how to optimize them, you can have successful dedicated landing pages for any occasion. Within those ad copy formats, there are a number of different landing page styles, which I'll outline here. The distinction between these pages that I'm about to describe lies in their call-to-actions. A landing page's positioning in your sales funnel – early on, mid-stage, or endgame – will determine what the page is asking the prospect to do.

Here are the most common types:

1. **Long-Form Sales Letter** – This landing page gets straight to the point with language that emphasizes making the order *now*. The end goal of the long form sales letter is to get this person to take action by purchasing a product via an online shopping cart or by calling. The call-to-action is generally a simple "call now" or "order now" with a listed tracking number or shopping cart order form. All-in-all, the long-form sales letter is the most easily-adaptable. It's highly informative, direct, specific, and effective. I personally like to start all campaigns with a *physical* long-form sales letter, even if I am not going to use this landing page format in my AdWords marketing. A long-form sales letter generally answers all of the questions a prospective buyer may have, and it includes all of the necessary information to make a sale and build a robust campaign.

2. **Product Positioning** – In this type of landing page, you're putting your product out there as being the best on the market. As examples, think of someone selling a toilet bowl or a water heater – always tangible items. You lead with a description of the problem and then introduce your product as the solution. You might want to include a *restricted time* direct offer or mention *limited supply* in order to increase urgency.

3. **Asset Positioning** – These landing pages are used generally near the start of a sales funnel. They are commonly referred to as opt-in pages and used in business to business (B2B) sales funnels. They offer an informational or demonstrative asset (often complimentary) in exchange for contact information. Some common examples include a "Buyer's Guide" e-book, a free report, or a sample kit. The bonus sections of this book, for instance, are strategically crafted opt-in pages.

4. **Service Selling** – For this type of landing page, you're generally selling speed and convenience. Think of a phone book offer: you're trying to get the person to make a risk-free call on a service they might need in order to help get your foot in the door. Offer a free quote, consultation, estimate, or means of scheduling service, and make yourself available to call.

5. **Event Invitation** – Again, this type of landing page generally occurs at the start of a sales funnel. Ask the prospect to join you at an Open House, or give them the URL of a webinar.

For every type of product or service you can think of, there is an ideal sales funnel. At the beginning, middle, and end of every successful sales funnel, there are *optimized landing pages*. Don't let your landing pages be anything but simple, user-friendly, and structured according to my proven-to-work formula. After all, landing page optimization is critical for your AdWords survival.

BONUS RESOURCES FOR "FINDING WATER"

Get Steve's Landing Page Survival Cheat Sheet ($49 value): This guide provides you with all of the built-in best practices you should incorporate into your landing pages. Following these 10 essential landing page tips will keep your pages converting again and again.

Receive a Complimentary Landing Page Review ($297 value): Access the experienced team that converts leads every day and get an in-depth analysis of your landing page performance.

Join Pay-Per-Click Prosperity – the place for better Google AdWords performance – and access this resource today.
Go to: payperclickprosperity.com

Chapter 5 Survivor's Summary

In this chapter, we learned the ins and outs of the most critical component of lead generation: dedicated PPC landing pages.

First of all, we covered definitions as well as the common misconceptions about landing page setup that result in wasted spend. We spent some time correcting the "5 Most Common Landing Page Mistakes" before transitioning into "The Basics of Landing Pages" and how to optimize them.

There are two primary formats for landing pages, and we referred to them as "The Pain Dynamic" and the "Challenge Assignment." Both structures follow the direct response ad arrangement, however one solves a challenge and the other creates interest. Steve provided a diagram and example of each. Finally, we ended the chapter by discussing the different styles of landing pages, which are determined by their call-to-actions.

Your takeaways from this chapter should be how to optimize a landing page and what a call-to-action is.

Test Your Survival Skills: *(Find answers on page 190)*

1. When attempting to attract the attention of a "Researcher," offering a free downloadable asset on your landing page might make them _____ likely to enter your sales funnel than offering a free in-office consultation.

2. Landing pages ought to be _____, meaning that the visitor is not expected to follow any other links or navigational paths other than to complete the call-to-action.

3. The fact that more than 2/3rds of Americans own smartphones makes it even more critical that every landing page you create is _____, meaning it can be seen by mobile search.

4. "Enter Your Mailing Address to Receive a Free Sample" is an example of a _____.

In Part II, we learned how to set ourselves up for success with intelligence reporting, how to speak directly to your ideal prospect, and how to optimize landing pages for maximum conversion. You're ready for everything!

Now we need to test those skills. In the next part, we'll apply strategies to launch your business to the top of the AdWords food chain.

Our primary focus in Part III will be to answer the following questions:

- **Is my current AdWords account hemorrhaging money, and if so, what can I do to stop it?**

- **How do I plan out my new Google AdWords budget?**

- **What can I do to outsmart my competition and dominate my market?**

This final part of the *Survival Guide* will cover the calculations, metrics, and techniques you can rely on from your first 90 days of AdWords to achieving your long-term PPC goals. Everything you need to transition from surviving to thriving is here, so grab your utility belt and let's go!

PART III: IT'S GO TIME

Discover Step-By-Step Proven Strategies You
Can Implement To Thrive In The AdWords Wild

6 | Using The First Aid Kit

7 Common Google AdWords Budget Bleeders and How to Fix Them

6.1 - How to Stop a Bleeding Budget

So you're fed up and frustrated with your Google AdWords experience. You feel like you are spending *uncontrollably*, and there's nothing you can do.

You are not alone. In fact, almost half of my clients come to me with some kind of baggage regarding AdWords because they feel Google has failed them. Still, they know they can't give up on what should be the #1 source of new clients, customers, or patients for their business. But with the broken down PPC campaigns they're running, they're hemorrhaging money, and the new leads aren't coming in at nearly the rate that they are bleeding out. They need some *Google AdWords first aid*, and that's what the adaptable advice in this chapter is all about.

I am here to tell you that there is something broken in almost 97% of all Google AdWords campaigns. There are a lot of moving parts, and everything has to be finely tuned to put your business in a position to win. So right here and right now I am going to explain to you:

- How you can drive in a consistent source of new leads at a cost that makes business sense.

- How you can take back control and put an end to the fear you have of Google maxing out your credit card with nothing to show for it.

- How you can turn clicks into customers and keywords into a reliable source of new revenue.

- How you can drastically improve your lead quality and expand your sales funnel.

First, let's check the damage.

How to Determine if You Have a Bleeding Budget

The most obvious sign of a bleeding budget is that your ad is receiving plenty of clicks but you are still not generating leads: a lack of conversion. You need valuable leads to balance out what you're spending and make your investment worth wile. And I don't mean soft leads like extended page views – I mean *hard leads,* specifically calls that end with sales or forms that contain contact information with prospects demonstrating illicit pain. I mean real prospective buyers and real cash to line your pockets. Having traffic to your site is great, but you need to remember that every click costs money. And if you aren't making that money back in revenue, well, then your credit card keeps getting charged without you really getting anything in return. You should be able to look at your investment at the end of a month and determine that your ROI was worth the spend…and that your next month's budget will assuredly cover its cost in sales as well.

Low conversion rates are the most common Google AdWords problem. Fortunately, they're often the fastest and easiest to fix. Take a look at your PPC campaigns – are they optimized? Where is this entire wasted ad spend coming from? Finding the root of the problem is half the battle.

What's Causing Your Bleeding Budget?

Here are seven common reasons a Google AdWords budget doesn't adequately turn out leads. Are you losing money every month?

1. **Ad Serving Campaign Settings:** When a campaign is established, you set a daily budget with Google. There are two types of ad delivery configurations within Google's campaign setup: "Standard" and "Accelerated."

Do you know which one your campaign is running? Do you know why? What's the strategy? Your ad delivery campaign settings may be incorrectly configured for your defined goals or market conditions.

The method you choose determines how fast your ads are served and how long your budget lasts throughout the day. The standard method will evenly distribute bids throughout the 24 hours. The accelerated delivery method will show your ads as fast and frequently as possible until you hit your daily budget, having (theoretically) captured all the opportunity and demand the market has to offer.

Here's how I like to think of it: when it's closing time at the bar, some people like to slow-sip their final drink of the evening to make it last– some people like to slam them down the hatch and carry on with their night. Either way, that one drink is all you get. Depending on your goals and your market, each of the ad serving strategies has distinct pros and cons for your budget's optimization.

Let's say you are a heating contractor in Buffalo – you rely on weather events, mainly severe blizzards, to drive in your leads. The standard ad delivery method will evenly distribute your ads during the day, and your ad may not appear at the times that matter the most (i.e. early in the evening when people get home from work and discover their furnace has shut down). You may be only getting just a handful of opportunities.

If a competitor uses the accelerated method and times his ads just right, he could have an explosive amount of leads in the same time period. Based on your business goals, the standard ad delivery method could actually be the root cause of your bleeding budget. All new campaigns within Google automatically default to this feature, so go check on which one your own PPC campaign is set for right now. Make sure it is in alignment with your goals.

2. **Keyword Strategy:** The wrong keyword strategy could open up the flood gates for all of the wrong kinds of traffic. That means more clicks with fewer leads – in other words, more investment with less return.

Google AdWords gives you the ability to choose keywords with laser-focus. To facilitate the building of your keyword strategy, Google allows you to choose from several "matching options." Let's explore those:

- Broad
- Broad Match Modifier
- Phrase Match
- Exact Match
- Negative Match

Optimizing keyword strategy is a critical part of running a successful Google AdWords campaign. Just one single keyword being improperly configured can throw off the entire formula! So we'll need to familiarize ourselves with these options and start investigating how we're currently using them to make our budget dollars count.

I like to go deep sea fishing, so I'll give you a fishing analogy. I'll spare you from having to listen to my fishing stories – that's what my next book will be for. For now, let's just try to stick to AdWords optimization.

In this analogy, you're fishing for quality leads. You want to go out and catch as many healthy fish as you possibly can. On a deep sea fishing boat, you're going to have a number of different tools to make different types of catches – in this case the keywords are your fishing tools.

Using the "broad" and "broad match modifier" keywords is like going fishing with a commercial-grade fishing net: it allows you to capture a large volume. By the same token, "broad" keywords get you a high degree of traffic. Yet the challenge with this is that those catches are still just *potential* quality leads. You end up casting a really wide net and getting plenty of fish, but most of them aren't the kind of fish you want. Some aren't edible, others are too small, and others just don't measure up to your criteria – so now you have to throw them back. "Broad" and "broad match modified" keywords do the same thing: they open up traffic to a very wide audience and allow the riffraff in.

To get more specific, we'll get literal. As an example of a business developing a keyword strategy, let's think of a fisherman in Puerto Rico who is renting out his boat to tourists for deep-sea fishing trips. In a broad keyword strategy, you would use the term *fishing*. Now, everybody who searches for *fishing* becomes an impression. However, the broad strategy would also open up the flood gates for traffic that would include non-relevant keywords like *Babel fish translator, office of fishing and wild life, how to cook blue fish, what are fish oils, Marine Fisheries, fishing gear pro shops*, et cetera, et cetera. This match type is certainly a budget bleeder if not managed correctly.

Moving on to the "phrase match modifier" – this option gives you much more control to help you attract a higher quality prospect. Think of the "phrase match modifier" keyword type as a fishing pole with a specific type of bait. This is a tool designed to catch one kind of fish. You catch one fish at a time, and you inevitably wind up throwing a few back in, but more or less you're getting a controlled source of fish and some quality bites – that is, traffic with some actual leads.

So, to revisit our fisherman example: phrase match strategy is the best option to drive in phrases or terms that would be directly relevant to his trade, such as *"Best San Juan fishing boat rentals," "San Juan fishing boat,"* and *"rent fishing boat in San Juan"* – all relevant keyword phrases that would trigger his ad so he can attract an ideal prospect to take action on an his advertisements. Phrase match is the best option to use when just starting out, as it will deliver less but more qualified traffic to your sales funnel, limiting your bleeding budget. If you aren't getting any bites, you may need to change your bait – do some research on search trends to find the keywords your prospects are searching for.

The next option is exact match. Think of exact match as the most conservative approach to attracting traffic. This is where Google offers you precision-based accuracy in defining your keywords and serving your ads.

In my fishing analogy, it's a lobster trap. You place it out at the bottom on the ocean, and you wait for the lobster to take the bait. It is the slowest but typically the most accurate way to attract very high quality traffic. There's very little waste involved, since there are very few clicks coming through who aren't directly interested in what you're selling. If you want to get even more specific, you can use this option for a "long-tail keyword." We'll discuss these some more later down the line, but I'll take the opportunity to define it here:

○ **Long-Tail Keyword** – The longer and more specific search terms that Google visitors are more likely to input when they are closer to purchasing a product or service.

In the phrase match example, you'll notice I placed quotation marks around my phrases. Google allows your keyword to include words both before and after the quotes, so in a phrase search, the term Best *"San Juan fishing"* boat would trigger an advertisement for my fisherman. The search inputs Cheap *"San Juan fishing"* and even Free *"San Juan Fishing"* would also trigger ads – and probably allow in a few low quality leads. In the exact match strategy, however, the keywords are placed inside of brackets, and only the exact term will cause an ad to appear. So [*San Juan Fishing*] would have to be the specific keywords typed into Google for the ad to show. This is the keyword strategy that completely prevents any wasted budget, since you are tightly controlling the flow of search.

The final keyword type is the negative match. I honestly can't think of a good fishing analogy for negative keywords here. I guess, depending on your fishing adventure, there are certain types of bait that attracts specific fish. So negative keywords could be the *"anti-bait."*

I'll be honest: I've never been very good with analogies.

Anyway, when you program terms like *cheap, free* or even *Babel* as "negative keywords" in your campaign, Google is instructed not to show your ads when they are used in search terms. Applying negative keywords to a campaign is an on-going refinement process. The more negative keywords you capture and install over time, the better and higher quality traffic you will generate. In the industries I work in, I maintain a proprietary list of negative keywords to give new clients a competitive edge, fast-tracking them years ahead of their competitors.

Can you think of negative keywords you can implement in your own campaign to steer away low quality traffic?

Take a look at your current keyword strategy – how well does it distribute strength between these different keyword matching types? Consider tightening that strategy to make the best possible use of each individual search so that as much of your traffic as possible can be feasibly converted into leads. It's about deciding which tools are going to get the job done, namely which keyword matches will capture the traffic that your business needs.

Which reminds me of this one time I was fishing in San Juan, and you wouldn't *believe* the size of this large-mouthed bass…

3. **Targeting:** The next most common way that small businesses bleed budget is by neglecting their AdWords targeting. Google gives you the ability to narrowly target the audience to whom you would like to serve ads. In the lead generation world, you can target by location – that includes cities, towns, zip codes, counties, states, and countries. There are even areas where you can target by specific neighborhoods. Google is constantly improving targeting options. It's to the point where I wouldn't be surprised if, someday, you could target *specific city blocks*. That's the direction that search is going in: hyper-localization.

    With AdWords' targeting function, you can create an advertising radius and exclude specific places. There are also new features that allow you to target your display ads by demographics such as ages and interests, so if you know that your ideal clients enjoy travel, you can setup a display advertisement campaign and just target this segment of your market using affinity profiling tools.

    Targeting is one of the simpler strategies you can implement to a campaign to control a bleeding budget. You would be surprised how many local businesses overlook this feature. My team and I routinely identify businesses who serve ads in markets thousands of miles away from their part of the country because the targeting feature was never used. Imagine if your local dentist was advertising to the entire United States! That would be insane, right? Well, I've seen worse.

Poor targeting is a very quick and reckless way to bleed a budget, but it should be a no-brainer during your campaign setup. Make sure your targeting is narrowly focused to the market you would most like to serve.

4. **Click Fraud and Malicious Behavior:** Whether your business is the new kid on the block or a major player planning to take leadership in your market, you are at almost certain risk of attracting malicious click behavior. I mentioned this in the "Technology" chapter: click fraud is where a competitor deliberately clicks on your ads in an effort to drive up your daily spend. Their clicks still cost you money from your AdWords budget, but obviously these viewers have no intention of buying or becoming leads. That right there is wasted ad spend – and it happens all the time.

    Of course, you would never do something like that, but I see it happen in almost *every single campaign* my team and I manage. In a local, competitive setting, the competitor who engages in this form of online vandalism is receiving no financial gain – he just does it with the intent of weakening his competition.

    Early on, Google really had no tools or technology to prevent, track, or manage this type of behavior. Today, the click fraud protection they offer is still very limited. They have a system named "invalid clicks" whereby they are able to identify malicious click activity, remove it from your account data, and give you a credit for those clicks using their algorithm...but, unfortunately, this is not an iron clad way to prevent click fraud from happening. Quite honestly, Google's click fraud technology is weak. Google tracks invalid clicks and often fails to distinguish properly between click fraud and legitimate customers who visit a site numerous times. The sheer amount of click fraud that slips through the cracks is stunning. As I said before, many users are losing hundreds, if not thousands, every passing month.

    That's why my company developed ClickOptix, our proprietary

conversion optimization and performance tracking technology: this software provides us with 100% transparency and comprehensive insight into every click our clients' advertisements receive. I've briefly described our click fraud protection before, but now I'll go into some more detail, since click fraud protection is immensely important to stop budget bleeding.

This is how it works:

Our click "accounting system" tells us exactly who is clicking on our clients' ads on the level of their IP address. The visit is time stamped and assigned a unique session ID. If for any reason the same visitor comes back and proceeds to click on another ad, we are able to quickly identify and take action against any malicious behavior – saving our clients thousands of advertising dollars over the course of the year.

Click fraud is still unfortunately a very real thing and needs to be carefully managed in a manual process. Every month, my team identifies high volumes of click fraud, and we are able to hold Google accountable by opening click fraud investigations. ClickOptix places a cookie on and tracks each independent visit from a specific IP address. We are able to track the origin of every visitor as well as their entire visit history. With this information, we can provide Google with the evidence they require for a client to receive click credits.

Most importantly, we are able to identify and isolate the IP address of the fraudulent user. Google gives you the ability to exclude specific IP addresses from ever seeing your ads again, and this is a great way to eliminate the bleeding budgets that result from click fraud once and for all. Imagine advertising in an "invisibility cloak" that protects you from enemies. You could be actively leading the pack in your competitive landscape, and your fiercest, most cut-throat competitors would have no idea since they would no longer see your ads. Let your competitors fight it out with each other – in the meantime, you can pull into the lead undetected!

5. **Technology Setup:** In the "Technology" chapter, I discussed how you should establish a foundation for success. Here's how not

having that valuable basis can directly cause you to lose money.

Speed is one thing you can't be shy of in the online advertising arena. The internet moves in minutes and seconds – by the time you have finished reading this sentence, there will have been tens of thousands of searches made across the globe. Consumers are conditioned for speed. They want information now, and they'll find that information on any device that suits them in the immediate moment – whether that's a mobile phone, a tablet, or a desktop computer. If you dedicate any sizable budget to online advertising, you can't be cheap about hardware and software. Faulty servers, a lack of web caching, and buggy web pages mean slower load times and lost opportunities.

Here are some examples of real life situations that can be avoided if you have the right equipment in place:

- You click on an ad and end up on a blank screen.

- You click on an ad, and it takes more than 15 seconds for the page to load. 15 seconds is a very long time nowadays for someone to stick around and wait for your site.

- You click on an ad on your mobile phone, and you are taken to a desktop version of your website where it is difficult to read the info.

- You click on an ad, and the website server is down. You go back the next day and the server is still down. A few days later the site is still down.

See, there is less than a 50% chance Google will shut down your ads for you if your server crashes, meaning that your ads will still be running and that people will be clicking on them only to end up in the abyss. Those dead-end clicks are costing you precious advertising dollars. What's worse is that you might not even know that your clicks are completely worthless if you aren't tracking your metrics comprehensively! Even if you do happen to visit your site while the server is crashed and discover the problem, what are you going to do? Who can you hold accountable? There's no telling when or if your server will go back up.

That's why, as an advertising agency, we invest heavily in the best hardware and security software for our clients. We have a built-in server disaster plan with redundancies, so if a server were to fail, their landing pages would automatically be fired up in a new location in real-time with no risk of ad spend loss.

Having deficient technology supporting your campaigns is an absolute budget bleeder – but it can and should be completely avoided by all of the people who read this book.

There are no excuses! This is a simple budget bleeder you can prevent starting *today*.

Again: rule out a bad technology setup as a budget bleeder and give yourself the opportunity to win by taking the steps necessary to deliver speed and relevancy to your prospects. In other words, don't cut corners! You'll never survive in the wilderness unless you find a safe place to camp.

6. **Ad Copy:** I already walked you through the 10 Rules of Writing Killer Copy in the "Ad Copy" chapter. Does your current ad copy measure up? Let's take a look.

   Once you have ruled out your campaign settings, keyword strategy, targeting, click quality, and technology as potential budget bleeders, the next place to look is in your ad messaging. Here are some questions you should consider before you start editing:

   - Is your ad copy driving in clicks and no leads?

   - Are you promising too much in your ad copy?

   - Are you baiting and switching – meaning are you serving ad copy that's "too good to be true" and then clarifying your message on the landing page with terms and conditions?

   - Is your ad copy relevant? Namely, does it match the keywords that trigger the ad?

   - Are you driving people to a landing page with the same message as your ad copy?

   - Are you positioning your very best offers, and are they unique compared to your competition?

If you are getting a really good click-through rate on your campaign but you are not converting leads, there is a good chance that calibrating your campaign with regards to one of the above questions will solve your problem. In my experience, almost 9 times out of 10, if you are getting a high CTR on your ad copy and the Google Quality Score is good throughout your ad groups, then the budget bleeder culprit is that you are not carrying your advertising message across to the landing page. Which brings me to our final budget-bleeder...

7. **Landing Pages:** Outside of working your ad copy and keywords into your landing page, one way you can increase your conversion is to make sure you have a dedicated landing page for each one of your ad groups.

Earlier, I spoke of the immense importance of landing pages to the survival of your campaign. Too many businesses make the mistake of running ads to the home page of a website – and too many other businesses make the alternate mistake of trying to have their landing pages do too much.

Landing pages are simple. Work in the advertising message, identify the prospect's pain or challenge, and solve it with benefits and a clear, concise call-to-action. Routinely split-test your landing pages, take the winning elements, and work them into other landing pages throughout your campaign.

Hard work? Absolutely.

Impossible? Absolutely not.

Putting that extra time into your landing pages will be worth the effort in budget that they save you. Remember the ROI! Stop those bleeding budgets by going back to the "Landing Pages" chapter resources to optimize your landing pages today.

When you follow these 7 tactical steps for troubleshooting your Google AdWords Campaign, you can easily turn a bleeding budget around into a profitable source of new business. Just know the signs, where to look, and how to adjust.

Now, back to that large mouthed bass...

BONUS RESOURCES FOR "USING YOUR FIRST AID KIT"

Register Now for this Webinar On-Demand: *Discover How to Increase Sales and Eliminate Google AdWords Budget Bleeders: Step-by-Step Proven Solutions to Get More For Less.* In this webinar, you will learn:

1. The 3 strategies you can implement today to increase your leads and cut back 20% of wasted ad spend.

2. How to outsmart your competitors and dominate your local market by taking advantage of Google's newest features.

3. The 4 things your pay-per-click manager won't tell you about your lead generation performance.

4. How you can get 100% visibility into key performance metrics and improve your results almost overnight.

Join Pay-Per-Click Prosperity – the place for better Google AdWords performance – and access this resource today.
Go to: payperclickprosperity.com

Chapter 6 Survivor's Summary

In this chapter, you asked yourself the question: does the return on my AdWords investment justify what I spend? Steve helped you find some answers.

Your takeaways from this chapter should be why your AdWords account is wasting money, the typical causes of budget bleeding, and how you can alter your current strategies to fix it.

Test Your Survival Skills: *(Find answers on page 190)*

1. The two types of ad delivery configurations within the Google AdWords campaign setup are _____ and _____.

2. A divorce law attorney in Portland, Oregon might use a _____ to ensure his ads don't appear for people searching for his service in Portland, Maine.

7 | Rationing Your Supplies

A Lesson In Google Math They Didn't Teach You In School

7.1 Understanding Google Math

Alright, we've covered a great deal, and at this point you might feel overwhelmed by the information I'm throwing at you. That's perfectly fine – in fact, it means you're doing a good job of absorbing all the details! To help in the process, I'm using this chapter partially as a summary.

But more than just a summary, this chapter's analysis is going to be about going back to where we were and doing some of what I call "back-of-the-napkin math" – simple number-crunching with hypothetical estimates to give you a sense of:

- The time-investment necessary for success.
- The profit margins in this venture you should pursue/expect.
- The potential ROI (return on investment) for the entire venture.

What does your budget for Google AdWords start at? What should it grow to? What should you be expecting in return? These are all the questions that relate to distributing your investment, i.e. *rationing your supplies*. Obviously, the exact numbers will vary based on the size of the business you're running, the market you're inhabiting, and a host of other limiting (and unlimiting) factors that only you can know for certain. However, these are the guidelines that have made me and my clients successful, and if you follow this framework, you can anticipate success as well.

With the right manager, Google AdWords can be pretty addictive. Sometimes, when I don't have my survival guide hat on, I refer to myself as "Google's drug dealer" for my long-term clients— because once you get a taste of what I deliver through PPC, you want more and more of it. I have worked with a large number of clients throughout the years where they started with a $1000 or $2000 budget per month, and I helped them successfully grow it to $10,000 to $20,000 in short order. You don't grow and scale a budget like that without having the math make sense.

A highway billboard costs the same regardless of how many drivers see it, but AdWords only costs money when people click. You aren't just paying for potential visibility – you pay for active consumer interest.

Now, remember: a growing Google AdWords budget doesn't just mean you're paying more – it means you're getting more clicks on your ads. Google AdWords is really the only advertising medium that charges based on results or, to put it another way, "consumption." However, the results in this scenario are clicks, which, as I've told you, are really just the beginning of lead generation. In order to reach that satisfactory ROI, you need to be organized and have all of your resources together so that those clicks that charged your AdWords budget are traveling through your marketing funnel and reliably becoming sales.

By now, I've covered what the 3 necessities for AdWords survival are. We've examined technology, ad copy, and landing pages, explained their importance, and shown you why the formulas work. Now it's up to you: for your business to be firing on all cylinders, you need to be constantly reworking, retooling, and keeping a pulse on your account – or, at least, have an AdWords manager whom you know can do all of those things for you. A lot of good things happen when you do PPC the right way. If you think the numbers you want are not obtainable, just read this chapter and I'll show you how to get there.

Getting Started: How to Develop the Right Budget

First and foremost, when you're starting with Google AdWords, especially if you are doing it on your own for the first time, you're going to want to kiss at least your first $500 to $1000 goodbye. Write it off as a cost of doing business. It is your investment in learning and understanding all of the concepts in this book. A good provider will be able to get you ramped up fast without a lot of waste in testing – especially if they understand the intricacies in your specific industry. That's why, even if I've already worked with others in the same industry, my company takes a deep dive into the markets of the clients we work with. We invest 60-90 minutes in an extensive kick-off call to get things down pat – and that's only the beginning. Through constant communication, we keep the cost of the learning curve down to a minimum.

One of the first questions I get is: "How much should I invest?" Sometimes I'll get a referral client who wants to spring right out of the gate – "So and so is spending $10k a month, and I want you to do the same exact thing right away." I appreciate the ambition, I really do. But you have to understand that growing a Google AdWords budget is a science: you can't succeed without collecting data first. I always recommend the *crawl, walk, run* approach. Piecing together a starting budget should be based on a few things:

1. **The cost of your average client acquisition** – How much does it cost you, on average and including all marketing resources, to acquire a new client, customer, or patient?

2. **Your client's long-term value (or LTV)** – There are two moving parts here: first, how long does your average client stay with you, and second, how much are they worth to you over the entire lifespan of the relationship? This requires you to estimate approximately how much the total price of your services with them is going to be in the long term.

If you know these numbers, then you are a master of understanding your business. You are most likely not interested in placing caps on performance – you know that you can spend the most in your market to acquire a new customer as long as you do not exceed the average cost of client acquisition. This is the first best practice of budget planning:

It's A Numbers Game

"What did you say Steve – *spend the most?*" some of you might say, "I thought that Google AdWords optimization was about spending the *least!*"

Most of your competitors are in the frame of mind that they need to spend as little as possible on acquiring new clients, customers or patients. That's because they are not considering the big picture, and they do not know their numbers. They treat marketing in their business as a luxury or an unnecessary expense. Most small businesses are not consistent in their marketing spend – they believe that their budget for advertising should be a fixed amount regardless of their revenue, or that they can skip certain months altogether. Theirs is a "Feast or Famine" approach wherein they increase ad spend on their best months and tighten their belt on your worst…but this only results in failure.

You can think of it like diet and exercise: if you go one week hardly eating at all and then the next week eating chocolate chip cookies with every meal, you're still going to be in pain, but you aren't going to see any results. Similarly, if you plan a rigid diet without consideration to your exercise, you'll wind up injured and with nothing to show for it. That's because dieting and marketing both require consistency, discipline, and dynamic scaling to work. They also require immersion: you can't just go part of the way.

That's why you need to know and understand your numbers so you can make smart and confident decisions.

When you are able to spend the most in your market to acquire a new customer, client, or patient, you will begin to dominate.

Now, I'm not saying you should plan to out-spend *yourself* here; quite the opposite. You need to find the sweet spot that allows you to outspend the unenlightened competition and still come away with solid ROI. If you don't know what your cost to acquire a new client is or the estimation of their long-term value, then you cannot take this approach yet. Do the back-of-the-napkin math and then come back. I'll still be right here.

The second budget best practice seems like a pretty simple rule, but it can get pretty complicated when you apply it. Again, though, you just need to do the math.

The Rule of 6/10/15 Percent

If you've been in business for a while, then there's a good chance you've heard of or even practice the method of applying a constant percentage of marketing spend against revenue goals. If you know you need to generate $50k in sales this month, what percentage of those sales are you willing to spend to hit this target?

- If you have a healthy, established business and you communicate to your clients, customers, and/or patients regularly, then you most likely do not have to exceed more than 6% of your revenue for your marketing spend.

- If you are a younger business with a smaller client base, then you're most likely somewhere in the middle – the 10% range.

- If you're in high growth mode (and don't care about process and consumer relationship building) then you're in the 15% range.

These numbers are generalized and based on my experience – you may find 4% or 8% may be the percentage of revenue you need for your marketing spend to achieve your targets. But this is the guideline to go by.

I'm assuming here that Google AdWords is not your only egg in the basket... it shouldn't be. You never want to solely rely on just one advertising source to drive in new business. Diversification is key. You will find, however, that Google will represent your lowest cost of client acquisition after direct referrals if you're doing it right. AdWords should also represent your fastest sales cycles and your overall best return on investment.

How do you know which bracket you fall into? Well, it depends on a number of things. Here are the top 3:

1. **Your capacity to service the sales** – Do you have enough skilled employees? Enough inventory?

2. **Whether or not you have an established client base you can sell to** – Do you have an up-to-date client database? How many people are on it?

3. **Your ability to actually close new opportunities** – When a call comes in, what is the historical probability of you making the sale?

Do the back-of-the-napkin math. When you do, apply the ratio and find the ideal rate of spend you should be investing in your Google AdWords.

At this point, some of you may be shaking your heads and saying to yourselves: "Steve, you have it all wrong – I can't spend a fixed rate on marketing because that won't be effective for me. My business is different!"

Well, sorry Charlie, but it's really not. If you disagree with any of the above, here are 3 questions to consider before you spend a dime:

1. What is My Plan to Bring on a New Client?

Let's assume you own a dental practice. You know there is a good chance you will lose new business to fear and uncertainty. I've seen it happen.

When I was a kid, I remember my dad being in agonizing pain from a toothache. It was *bad*. My dad doesn't drink, nor did I grow up with alcohol in the house – but that night my dad sat at the kitchen table with a bottle of brandy because it was the only way for him to settle down and temporarily soothe the pain. But he still didn't want to go to the dentist. My dad *fears* the dentist.

The next day, my mom set him up with an emergency appointment with an oral surgeon. He was scheduled to get that tooth pulled. It was a dramatic scene, and I joke about it with my parents to this day just because of the lengths she had to go to in order to get my dad in that chair.

Here was her patented "tough love" way of forcing him to get the procedure: she drove him a few cities over to the appointment, and once he got to the office and (as predicted) refused to go in, my mom told him that meant he had to walk home – which was at least 10 miles away. This was before cell phones existed, so there was no cab to call or Uber to pick him up. Pretty extreme, right?

But my dad's stubbornness was on a whole other level of extreme. He managed to pull his own tooth out and end his pain on his walk home.

Now, the oral surgeon had no idea this was happening. He most likely assumed, "Oh well, another cancel" and went about his day. What really occurred there was that there was somebody so unwilling to get in his chair due to fear and anxiety that he pulled out his own tooth and walked ten miles to avoid it. So, with my dad's story in mind, let's talk about the capacity to service new clients:

Welcoming and Reinforcement: Once you acquire a new customer, client, or patient, there is still a very good chance of losing them very early in the relationship. This applies for any marketing source. That's why you need to welcome them to the family.

This can be done a number of different ways. I greet clients with a welcome gift valued at over $500. The box contains a "Welcome to the Family" gift, a letter thanking them for their business, a description of what they should expect in their first 90 days, and instructions on how to conduct business with my company. Inside, they receive a Frequently Asked Questions list that addresses the most common concerns or objections they may still have – even after the sale has been made. This process has almost guaranteed I won't lose a client in the time frame when it matters most: during the "honeymoon" period.

Remember, you will always have "loose ends" once a sale is completed. Things happen and people change their minds. Knowing what the customer's LTV is will help you estimate what you should spend in order to make them stay.

If email existed back when my dad was in pain the way it does today, the oral surgeon could have put together and sent him a video welcoming him to his practice. The content could contain a message about what to expect during the visit and could have very easily addressed his concerns. What can you do to welcome and reinforce your company's message?

Speed and Timing: Once customers, patients, or clients purchase from your company, how fast can you deliver the product or service? There's a good chance if the oral surgeon offered emergency service, my dad could have gone to the dentist that night instead of sitting in the kitchen drinking brandy. He would not have sat in pain and thought about all of the horrible things the dentist would do to him. Be there during the worst of the pain, and they'll be there in your office!

Doing the Work: Typically, the easiest part of this whole plan is doing what you're good at and fulfilling the requirements of the job. That's why it's important not only to deliver the work, but also to do so in a way that builds a long-term relationship.

For example, when I purchased my last car, the finance manager gave me a 3-year supply of free oil changes: that's some great reinforcement. Every time I come back, they also give me a place to do my work, free snacks, free coffee, and a free car wash with detailing. As a company, this dealership knows its LTV. They can afford to give away the free stuff and build this ongoing relationship because they know I will (A) refer their business to my friends and family, (B) keep coming back for service, and/or (C) purchase my next vehicle from them.

What's a few free cups of coffee in comparison to the cost of a new car?

2. How Large is My Database, and How Often Do I Communicate?

Once you build a relationship, you've already made the investment in acquiring the new customer, client or patient. But much like a successful marriage, it takes work to keep the magic going.

That's why it is important to *stay in front of them*. Not in a pointless, annoying, or stalker-ish kind of way, but in a way where you can deliver value. Once they do business with you the first time, no matter how awesome the experience was, you're still not Coca Cola, Disney, or Ford. That means there's a very good chance a month from now they will have forgotten your name (unless, of course, they had a bad experience. The psychology behind that could be a book in itself).

So how do you keep the momentum going? How do you stay in front of your best clients, customers, and patients?

For me, I like to go old school: I use the power of printed newsletters. There's something special about getting mail, and there's something even more special when it comes once a month. If you know your LTV, then you can figure out the cost of what you would get in return by engaging in this type of relationship marketing.

3) What is My Sales Process?

Let's assume you own a heating and cooling company, and you sell and install central air conditioning systems. You know it's a numbers game: you need X amount of appointments and will generate Y sales with your comfort sales consultant. Your best guy may close 50% of sales, which means the other 50% did not purchase from you. You can punch in more sales by following up on all of the open opportunities that did not close. You can come up with a series of phone calls, a series of direct mail postcards and emails, or a combination of calls and mail to chase after the business that was left on the table. A systematic follow-up campaign – even if it only collects 5% of open opportunities – can deliver a huge ROI and make the difference in how aggressive you get in your Google AdWords budget management.

Now, instead of an HVAC company, imagine your own business in the first sentence and read the paragraph again. What did you find? Did the equation still work? I'll bet it did.

Marketing is marketing is marketing. There's no reason these strategies won't work for your business or anyone else's. Most business owners are still trying to feel their way through marketing blindly, but those gut feelings aren't always right. Others just don't want to believe that their business model is compatible with this approach. They want to think that their business is different, that they can get away with cutting corners and still make the same revenue. Those are the companies that lose out in the end. You don't want to be that kind of marketer – you want your *competitor* to be that marketer! Do the math, follow my proven formula, and make AdWords work.

By asking yourself these questions, you can see that once you nail down these pieces of your business you'll have more confidence and better clarity in making budget decisions.

How To Prevent Budget Starvation: Solve for X

The third budgeting best practice is based on the capacity of your business. It's the Solve for X equation, and I'll show you how it works.

Let's assume you own a residential plumbing company with three service trucks. Each technician on your truck needs three booked service calls each for the day. That means if Google AdWords was your only source of leads, you would need 11 calls to come by way of AdWords into your organization.

"Steve – something's not quite adding up here! 3 trucks at 3 calls per day equals 9, not 11."

Well, here's the formula in this example broken down:

- AdWords management: delivers 11 calls at X per call
- Your customer service center needs to hit a booking rate of 80%
- 80% at 11 calls is 9 booked calls
- Your average ticket is $800
- Daily sales is $800 x 9 calls = $7200 in sales or $2400 per truck

Lots of back-of-the-napkin math there! Let's dig into it:

Notice the importance of the 80% booking rate. If the rate were 50%, you would need 18 calls — which, at $64.45 apiece, would make your marketing spend jump to nearly $1,200 (i.e. over 16% of revenue).

If you maintain your average marketing-to-revenue ratio at 10%, you can afford to spend (in this example) $7200 at 10%, which equals $720 per day. This is calculated as: $7200 (Total Sales) at 10% (Marketing Spend Rate) which equals $720 (Marketing Spend) divided by 11 (total calls).

You're looking for a $65.45 cost per raw call to your organization.

This is a great way to model out a daily, weekly, monthly, quarterly budget. All too often, I see local business owners making the mistake of locking themselves in and trapping their success by trying to do too much with limited budget. That's no way to survive with Google

AdWords. When you're stranded out at sea, you ration your supplies and you eliminate waste – but you don't just *not eat*, otherwise you won't have the energy you need to keep going! Budget starvation is not the answer. Eventually, when you can handle the capacity, you increase your budget and spend more to get more leads in return – this is how you grow your business.

In the example above, if the company works 20 days per month at 9 calls per day, they require 180 booked calls per month, meaning that their PPC manager needs to generate 225 raw calls at the 80% booking efficiency. If the cost per call is $65.45, then this company needs to plan on roughly a $15k monthly budget to sustain this level of call activity.

Sometimes this kind of math can be sobering. While it's still without a doubt the best and most dynamic form of marketing out there today, Google AdWords is not the get-rich-quick scheme some people treat it as. It requires time, effort, and financial investment. But when you understand your numbers and put in those 3 ingredients, you can expect to succeed.

7.2 - Keeping Score

Let's break it down further and discuss who should be responsible for what in your organization, because we are just scratching the surface here in what is measurable and which data points can help you make intelligent business decisions. In fact, there are over a dozen inflection points you can measure, and if you keep score for each component then you will know your outcome. Let me walk you through each one:

PPC Manager Inflection Points

1. **Impressions:** The total amount of your views your ad receives.

2. **Clicks:** The total number of actions prospective clients take by clicking on your ad.

3. **Click-Through Rate:** The percentage of impressions divided by clicks. Typically for me, a high click-through rate is the result of a highly effective ad and mature campaign. Different keyword

strategies and ad copy split-testing will impact click-through rate. As I mentioned in an earlier chapter, a really good campaign can become a *great* campaign with doubled lead volume by increasing your click-through rate by just one percentage point.

4. **Spend:** This is the total advertising budget invested during the specific time frame.

5. **Raw Calls Delivered to the Organization:** This is very simply the total number of unique calls your call center receives. Make sure to strip out duplicate callers or repeat calls. My call-tracking system automatically does this.

6. **Click-to-Call Conversion:** To get this measurement, you will need to measure your calls using a call-tracking program. Take all unique raw calls into an organization for a given day, week, or month and tally up the total number of clicks for the same time period. Divide the total number of calls by clicks. This number will give you a percentage for how effective your landing pages are. If you got 50 calls off of 100 clicks, your campaigns are converting at 50%! Congratulations: you have an impressive campaign.

As a company, my team and I track all of these core metrics in real-time for our clients using our ClickOptix technology.

You are going to find all kinds of conversion rates out there posted as "averages." Quite honestly, there is no industry standard reporting outlet to say, "This is the norm." I will tell you my closest competitors are proud of 6% conversions, which quite frankly suck. I have clients who routinely convert at a range between 30 and 70% – it depends on the market and the campaign. Whatever that number is, though, you need to be familiar with it. If you're not getting the conversion you want, you need to drill into the other metrics to figure out what is broken.

7. **Cost Per Call:** This is your total spend divided by unique calls into the organization. If your conversion is high, then this number should be at a reasonable level.

All too often I get asked the question: "How much does it cost businesses per inbound call with Google AdWords?" It really doesn't work like that. When you are in a direct-billing relationship, Google charges you for clicks, not calls, so the name of the game is to get as many calls out of the clicks as you can, which is determined by your conversion. If you suffer from low conversion, then you are going to have a high cost per call, which means there's something that can be improved in your strategy. Average cost per call varies between industries and markets, but you can always go to the best practice formula above and solve for X with your own business's numbers to find out what your goal needs to be.

These are the critical inflection points you need to hold your PPC manager accountable for in order to develop some sort of performance standard. There are a hundred other metrics you could introduce into the equation, but none that really serve any purpose other than what these cover – so don't waste your PPC manager's time. Remember, their time is your money.

For example, I once had a client for whom I managed an emergency heating campaign with a site conversion of 70%. The client was convinced the campaign could improve if I focused lowering his high "bounce rate" – a metric he pulled from his landing page inside Google Analytics. By Google's definition, a prospect who only visits one page on your website is considered a "bounce" if they don't go on to a new page – even if they pick up the phone and call you! In some industries, especially if you offer emergency service, a high bounce rate with good conversion is actually a *sign of success*.

So the point I'm trying to make here is to focus on your click to call conversion – that's all that really counts in the lead generation game.

Customer Service Representative Inflection Points

Once your PPC manager delivers the calls, it's up to your call center to qualify and book them. This is one of the most critical areas of the business, and it is often the most overlooked. Before you spend a dime on Google AdWords, you want to get the call process down pat, which includes not compromising on any of the following items:

- A live answer
- Solid phone script
- Objection handling sheets or cards

- An escalation point plan (i.e. an available manager who a call center rep can have take over in the event a lead goes sour).

There's a lot of psychology here. You want to practice, practice, and practice some more with your call center. When it comes to bad calls, I've seen it all, and I continue to see unique problems every month. Calls that go to a third party answering service where they place your prospect on hold for 5 minutes, calls that go to voicemail, calls where you have a customer service rep who has been with you for 20 years who likes to solve problems over the phone but not to book calls, so on and so forth.

Needless to say, there's a lot that can go wrong.

Your customer service team or call center reps are your offensive line, and their performance needs to be measured by the following metrics:

1. **Booking Rate:** How many raw calls did they receive, and how many were booked?

2. **Drop Rate:** How many calls were booked, and how many fell off? This inflection point is a marketing challenge that can be solved with a reinforcement campaign.

3. **Cost Per Booked Appointment:** Take the total investment with Google and divide it by the total number of calls you booked – this is your cost per booked call.

Then, once you hand off the booked call to your sales team or the person responsible for fulfilling the product or service, you should hold them accountable to these performance metrics:

Sales Person Inflection Points

1. **New Opportunities** – The total number of booked calls that resulted in a new opportunity.

2. **Closed Opportunities** – The total number of opportunities that resulted in a new sale or transaction.

3. **Total Sales** – Total closed sales.

4. **Average Transaction Size** – The total sales divided by closed opportunities.

Once you master Google Math, get the right PPC manager, nail down your call center, and construct a winning sales team, then you can move towards an unlimited budget. Your PPC success will be consistent at all levels of your business, and your ROI will have infinite upward potential.

BONUS RESOURCES FOR "RATIONING YOUR SUPPLIES"

Get Steve's "3 Legged Stool of AdWords Success" worksheet ($97 value): Built with more than 20 business metrics, this simple and easy tool will help you figure out how many leads your organization needs and how much you should budget for when launching a Google AdWords campaign. You will see directly how slight improvements in PPC management, call center management and sales management can impact revenue with this smart tool.

Get Steve's Pay-Per-Click Scorecard ($97 value): This powerful management template gives you the ability to measure and track 14 key performance metrics that impact your Google AdWords return on investment. Use it to track your core AdWords, call center, and revenue inflection points and tie them back to your spending to determine if and how your budget is bleeding. This tool allows you to collect data over time so you can keep a pulse on your month-over-month averages.

Join Pay-Per-Click Prosperity – the place for better Google AdWords performance – and access this resource today.
Go to: payperclickprosperity.com

Chapter 7 Survivor's Summary

In this chapter, Steve demonstrated how to structure a monthly Google AdWords budget. We learned how to start off with the right expectations, and we covered the 3 best practices of PPC budget management: the Numbers Game, The Rule of 6/10/15, and How to Solve for X. You did some back-of-the napkin math to calculate your ideal investment-to-profit ratio. We learned how to value customers based on their life-time value (LTV).

Finally, Steve broke down the inflection points for team performance. This included 7 metrics for PPC management, 3 for Call Service Representatives, and 4 for Sales Team success. That's 14 inflection points total to monitor and constantly improve! Use these to ensure every component of your AdWords lead generation system is operating at max efficiency.

Your takeaways from this chapter should be your target ROI and how you should plan for reliable client acquisition.

Test Your Survival Skills: *(Find answers on page 190)*

1. The two most important variables in determining your starting budget are _____ and _____.

2. Say you use 10% of your revenue for marketing. If your AdWords management delivers 15 calls, and you book them at a rate of 66%, and your average ticket size for those booked calls is $500, what should your raw cost per call be?

3. Improving _____ should be your main focus for every ad campaign you run, as this is the success metric that counts the most in the lead generation game.

4. Your CSR's _____ is determined by the percentage of raw calls they received that resulted in scheduled service.

5. Your salesperson's total sales divided by their closed opportunities is their _____.

8 From Surviving To Thriving

21 Proven AdWords Strategies to Outsmart Your Competitors and Get More For Less

8.1 - 5 Causes of Google AdWords Failure And How To Turn The Tide

So you've arrived at the final chapter of the *Google AdWords Survival Guide*.

Excited?

You should be, because this is where you will learn the serviceable techniques to help you reverse the dynamics and supercharge your advertising efforts. At the end of this chapter, you'll find the assistive resources from the entire book in one convenient package, plus some additional content geared towards taking leadership of your market with AdWords: you're getting a free offer to try out Pay-Per-Click Prosperity for two months where you will receive my newsletter and have access to exclusive tools, training and live group calls. This is the turning point where you go from being lost in the AdWords wild and prey to the reseller sharks to feeling like a natural PPC predator with the ability to dominate your market share. We've been honing our survival instincts and taking stock of our environment since page 1, and now it's time for you to thrive.

It really doesn't take much time to launch Google AdWords. Anybody who signs up for an account can do it. You can setup a campaign, draw a circle around the territory you'd like to generate leads from, think up a few keywords, and write your ad – no real barriers to entry there. A lot of local businesses do exactly that, or they hire a PPC management company and that's all they get.

But that's really all it takes to make a Google AdWords account: sign in and start paying. You may even have a pretty good short-term run at pulling in some leads...until you start to experience the following:

1. **Your competitors identify you as the new kid on the block, and they start clicking on your ads to size you up.** These clicks still cost money, but your competitors obviously have no intention of becoming leads or making purchases.

2. **The market starts to outbid you, and your ad positioning weakens.** By the second half of the month, the honeymoon is over. The market has caught on to your keyword and bid strategy, and it starts moving in. Your ads start to experience ad fatigue and eventually go lame.

3. **Somebody comes along and positions themselves with better ad copy.** Not all copy is created equal! If someone else knows how to appeal to the ideal customer better than you, you'll be lost.

4. **You start paying premiums for clicks that could have cost pennies on the dollar if managed correctly.** This goes all the way back to our AdWords "Sharks" chapter: if your PPC company has you in a no-refunds contract, manages your account with a software algorithm, and is charging you directly from your ad spend, then you need to get out ASAP.

5. **Frustration sets in.** Performance comes to a complete grind and you start to bleed budget. You lose confidence in Google AdWords, throw your hands up in the air, and give up completely. We've all been there before.

That's why it pays to have someone on your side who can help you make sense of it all and manage your account to best practices. If you have a rock-solid agency helping you, and they hold themselves accountable to AdWords perfection, it may be the one investment you make this year that truly pays for itself.

A good PPC manager can trim the fat off your campaigns, identify pockets of opportunity where you can generate leads at rock-bottom prices, and give you a competitive edge to aggressively win in your local market place.

There is a lot that goes into a successful Google AdWords campaign, and in this section I'm going to walk you through how my team and I manage our client accounts. These are the 21 strategies that have brought me to my current position as an expert PPC consultant. These practices are field-tested, formulaic, and *proven to get results*. With these plays, you can stop sinking and start swimming. This is how you go from surviving to thriving in the AdWords world.

First, we'll set the ground rules – or, in this case, the ground rule. Get ready for some more back of the napkin math, because this is the basic time-to-money ratio that I've used to get to the level of expertise I'm at today.

The Rule of "$53,000 to One"

You've heard me say a few times already that Google AdWords is a manual application. Of course, there are technologies you should have to give you a competitive edge, and my team and I use our own proprietary tools for tracking (ClickOptix, as I've described) – however, at the end of the day, the decisions impacting revenue performance should not be left up to a machine. You need a human there to drive the account in the right direction.

I've worked with many automation software applications in my day, and most of the good ones are designed for e-commerce – i.e. selling stuff online. The principles I will lay out here in this chapter are really designed to help you generate leads, not shopping cart transactions. As such, they require that you have a *person* at the helm of your campaign, which means planning out what your man-power investment needs to be.

So let me introduce you to my $53k:1 principle:

There are 160 work-week hours in a given month. My PPC managers will typically invest 3 man-hours per month for every $1000 we manage for our clients. This means if you invest a $5,000 budget with Google, we're allocating roughly 15 man-hours in labor to manage your account to our best practices each and every month. Take the maximum work-week hours in a given month, 160, and divide that by 3 man hours, and you'll see each of my PPC specialists is charged with managing $53,000 in total advertising spend per month.

That's one qualified, certified, and heavily trained PPC specialist for every $53,000 of budget.

Given that my average starting client invests around $5k per month, I need to keep my staffing levels at 11:1 – for every 11 clients, I have one PPC specialist managing daily performance metrics. This staffing rule sets our standard of excellence for service delivery and provides the foundation for the absolute best in Google AdWords account management and performance. Every day, we strive to deliver not only the best performance but also the very best service in our field. Overwhelming my team with any ratio larger than this one would result in poorly performing accounts, missed opportunities, and unhappy clients. And yet, you'd be surprised how many PPC companies aren't even close to this level of attention, expertise, or head count. Some of the publicly traded resellers have one kid fresh out of college running *hundreds* of PPC accounts at once.

Or maybe you wouldn't be surprised, depending on where you're coming from.

Remember when we talked about the importance of having *differentiators* to set your business model apart? Well, this is one of mine. At this level of staffing, service, and support, I'm able to differentiate my team and I as the service leaders. I give clients an AdWords management relationship that they *simply don't get anywhere else.* And because of this level of service and support, I am able to provide my clients with a no-strings-attached, contract-free way of conducting business. That's what makes my company the absolute best in the industry: all of my clients enjoy total transparency, cutting-edge technology, superior service, and guaranteed performance.

A lot of what makes this proposition so appealing, as you may notice yourself, is the transparency I offer my clients into the performance metrics of their accounts. The effectiveness of that transparency starts with knowing what to expect.

8.2 - 21 Proven Strategies for Outsmarting The Competition

Depending on the size of the local market and industry, it generally takes us roughly 5 to 15 days to launch a new campaign for a new account the right way. This is the most critical time for us to put our heads down and prepare our client for long term success.

This is where the 21 strategies come into play.

Each and every time you initiate an AdWords campaign, there's a performance threshold. You need to know that performance threshold: what numbers are you aiming for, and does your established presence have the capacity to make it there? Once you reach the threshold, you implement the next stage, which creates a new threshold to reach and surpass. It all goes back to my escalating approach: *crawl, walk, run.* First you cut ties with the AdWords managers who don't have your back. Then you organize a setup with the proper security, capabilities, and technology foundation. Then you start to plot out your campaigns, track how well they do, and make adjustments until your AdWords account is steadily producing revenue. Then you kick it into gear with marketing strategies that turn the game completely on its head. Then you start exercising the control over your business and your area that PPC is capable of delivering. Reach one threshold, and then start planning for the next one. All along the way as you are growing your business, these 21 strategies will give you a competitive edge.

I'm going to tell you how my team does it – keep in mind that my methods are dramatically more time-intensive than most companies. Additionally, some of these practices extend beyond the introductory phase and into your long-term strategy. However, my way is the only real way to optimize Google AdWords and to guarantee a consistent ROI. This is the effort that directly translates into results.

So without further ado, here are 21 ways we calibrate your campaign as a new client, the strategies you should apply *regardless* of who manages your PPC:

1. **Constant Communication:** Every single lead we generate for

you is reviewed. All of our clients have access to call-tracking technology, which is shared with the PPC manager assigned to their account. Within the call-tracking technology, you can tell exactly what happened on the inbound PPC call and determine its disposition. At this point, we are evaluating the lead quality and making adjustments as needed.

2. **Hourly KPI Monitoring:** I've taken you through the core performance metrics we manage each account by. At random, we choose a day during the first week when your account goes live. Your PPC manager will monitor and collect performance data on the hour. This gives us an idea of how well your campaign performs and how prospects react to your ads based on the time of day. The hour-by-hour snapshots of your account are critical in understanding how you stack up against others we are managing in the same industry. By this stage, we are able to make bid, ad copy, and landing page adjustments.

3. **Branded Campaigns:** One of the first campaigns we launch is the one that protects your brand. We place a low bid on your company name search terms to help us identify existing clients who may be searching for you. Additionally, this protects any of your offline investments: people who hear you marketing on the radio or in a newspaper ad may respond by Googling your company name, so it's important to be the immediate top result in order to capture that lead.

    Creating a branded campaign is a smart way to protect the leads you're already generating, and it prevents any risk of your brand accidentally creating a lead for a competitor.

    If you plan on going it with Google for the long haul and you're in a competitive market, you should consider officially trademarking the name of your business. Your shrewder competitors will quickly learn to bid on your company name directly, thereby driving up your CPC and stealing what should be your easiest leads. To prevent them from doing so, it is a best practice to have a registered trademark. In the AdWords Terms and Conditions, Google prohibits intellectual property infringement by advertisers. So let's say you're Burger King–

you can't just go out and run a campaign for the keyword "McDonald's," because that's a registered trademark. That campaign keyword would not be approved.

The same rule applies to infringements on copyrights. If someone goes out and completely rips off one of your landing pages or sales copy, there may be legal consequences, since this behavior is prohibited by Google's Terms and Conditions.

If you ever run into a copyright infringement situation, Google AdWords has a process by which you can file a trademark or copyright investigation. However, if you don't have your company name trademarked, you'll be leaving yourself open to plagiarism and fraud. If you can prove you have a trademark, there's a good chance the culprit will be swiftly penalized.

4. **Competitor Campaigns:** The next thing we do during our building process is build out a competitor campaign. Without violating trademarks, we essentially compile a list of all of your competitors and create minimal bids on their names and terms.

This is exactly why you want to trademark your brand. Competitors who understand how to optimize PPC will be doing this, and you want to take away that option for them wherever possible.

But we don't make competitor campaigns to be unethical or aggressively competitive – my team would never institute advertising principles that go against our client's requests or violate Google's Terms and Conditions. No, the reason we do this is so we don't overpay for clicks that would have otherwise went to your competitors – i.e. their existing clients, telemarketer calls, etc. You can completely avoid these calls by bidding a nickel on their name.

When AdWords registers that you have bid on your competitor's name, it gets ready to show the ads for that keyword. However, since the bid is just a nickel, it will give those results an appropriately low positioning – in other words, it will never really be visible for people to click. When someone searches for your competitor's name, then, you will not show up. You will never waste money by having returning customers for your competitors mistakenly click your ads.

To use an example, let's say you're an orthodontist in San Diego, and your competitor's name is Dr. Gold Orthodontistry. If an existing client of Dr. Gold searches for "Dr. Gold Orthodontistry San Diego," it's possible that your ads would show up since you most likely are bidding on San Diego Orthodontistry. In this case, you don't want this person to click your Google ads, because they are just going to turn around once they realize they're in the wrong place, and you'll still pay for the click. However, if you bid 1 nickel on the keyword "Dr. Gold Orthodontistry," your ads will never show up on those searches, and you'll never have to pay for bad clicks. You literally won't pay a cent. This helps cut out quite a bit of fat and potential loss of budget in the long term.

NOTE: Google prohibits having a trademarked competitor's name in your ad copy, so you never want to write ads that call them out. It's against their terms of service and a poor strategy anyway.

5. **Negative Keywords:** As soon as we launch our new campaigns, we set to work supporting them with an extensive list of negative keywords. Negative keywords drastically increase lead quality and help bring your campaigns soaring towards optimal performance. During the build process, as I've discussed, we review lead quality by listening to your calls and reviewing keyword data – from those initial findings, we begin the process of ongoing negative keyword placement to root out the low quality leads and non-relevant clicks your business gets.

6. **Click Fraud:** Most click fraud happens early on in a campaign – usually because, when you're with me, you are taking away *somebody else's* calls. Generally, it's the company that has been sitting in prime position for a while. Now you're the new kid on the block, and you're stealing away the current market leader's business – so he tries to knock you down a peg. But that sort of thing does not fly when you work with my team. We begin the process of identifying malicious click fraudsters, file click fraud

investigations with Google to receive credits, and completely eliminate the vandal's IP Address from ever seeing your ads again.

7. **Ad Timing**: During the first few days of a new campaign, we identify timing trends and answer the question, "When are the best times of day and days of the week to run our client's ads?" To go a step further, we also look into, "Are there certain messages we should be advertising in the morning versus the afternoon or at night?"

Imagine if you were only advertising in the pockets of time that really counted, the sweet spots in web traffic patterns where you could rely on attracting interested buyers. Ad timing is a great strategy to maximize ROI and develop really high quality leads. Like any other market, there are specific buying behaviors in your industry – there is a percentage of business that you can count on coming in from a specific time of day and day of the week.

Think about it: if you own a home, you probably discuss the upcoming week's errands and things to do with your husband or wife. In my home, this is called a "Honey Do" List. You typically start working on this list in the beginning parts of the week, like on a Monday or Tuesday. If you completely forget about something, you rush on Friday to tie up loose ends – this stage is called the "Honey Do This RIGHT NOW" List, and mine tends to be pretty long. So if I need to hire an electrician to come out and take care of an exterior light fixture that's not working, I am most likely going to perform my research and make the call on a Monday, Tuesday or Friday around lunch time – when I have a free moment at the office to work on personal items.

I bet you realize that you're about the same way.

With my ClickOptix software, my team tracks calls by time of day and by day of week. This helps us work with our clients who run 'round the clock campaigns by drilling into them and developing strategies to help push the needle when it matters most. We typically refer to this strategy as "day parting."

8. **Ad Placement and Bid Strategy**: As part of the ad timing strategy, we begin working on ad placement in your market. There's a lot that goes into this. As I've explained, ad placement on the Google search results page is determined by your bid amount and your ad's Quality Score for a specific keyword. Maintaining a prime or top-of-page position in your first week can bleed out quite a bit of budget with limited results, so we prefer to inch our way to the top taking the *crawl, walk, run* approach. The value of ad position is relative to the sales process and transaction size.

For transactions with low cost and high service speed, you want to have the higher positioning that gets you the best conversion. Being at the top of the list is like being the first phone book ad in your category – remember, you want to be the first guy to pick up the phone.

If your transaction is a large dollar amount and requires a sales process, you generally want to be positioned on the right hand side. People self-select when they're engaged in a buying process, and you will most likely end up with a better result by being placed in the 3rd, 4th, or 5th slot.

As I'm sure you picked up when I spoke about it before, it can take a lot of effort and research to gauge exactly where a person's eye will land when the search results load. It is a very exact science. There have been countless heat map studies out there you can research to see exactly how people interact with the ad section of Google – I included some in the "Ad Copy" chapter. You may have heard this from someone (or you may believe this yourself): *"My clients are too smart to click on the ads."* You would be surprised about how many people actually click on ads versus the organic results section – after all, AdWords didn't become Google's primary source of revenue out of nowhere. It's not a matter of smart and dumb, it's a matter of how well your sales copy is constructed and what value the customer stands to gain.

9. **Understand your Competitor's Call Flow**: Usually, your competitors are their own worst enemies. They create all kinds of obstacles for themselves to book calls. It's possible that you

used to be like them before you picked up your *Survival Guide* – but we'll skip the nostalgia.

You want to identify where your competitors are falling short and position yourself to reap the benefits. Here are two examples of competitor oversights that a sharp user will take advantage of:

- They are advertising after their business hours.

- They send callers to a voicemail box or answering service where it takes 5-7 rings before the machine fields the call.

In both cases, the competitor is frustrating his callers by making them wait. Take the opportunity to be the advertisement positioned right after your competitor during after-hours time, and be prepared to answer the call on the first ring.

Most people will call around and prefer to speak to a live person immediately. I have heard hundreds of callers from my own clients give in and hang up once they are directed to a voicemail or have had to sit on hold for a long period of time. You have only a 10% chance of booking a call if you're setup like this today. They'll bail on you, and it costs you a click. In fact, the CPC may have cost you *even more* than what it would cost to have a live person answering the call on the other end in certain markets, not to mention the fact that you're losing the value of the lead. Eradicating these bad business policies is critical to your success.

10. **Understand Your Competitors' Pricing & Discounting Structure:** Most discounting is artificial in nature, and a lot of your competitors most likely have weak discounting positioning that fails to build any sort of value. Some businesses even place barriers to entry by qualifying too hard when a quality prospect actually calls. Here's a real life example:

Recently, I took on a plumbing client who received a call where the prospect on the other end indicated that his water bills were extremely high, and he suspected he had a leak under his home beneath the slab. The call taker was instructed to qualify callers with a $59 dispatch fee. The prospect knew he had a serious problem – and in the plumbing world, slab leaks can easily be a $10,000.00 job. The prospect was not shopping on price. He just wanted to understand his options. The job would be expensive enough, so he would understandably rather not pay a fee for every consultation. He invited the company to come out, assess his situation, and provide him with an estimate. But the call taker hammered him hard on the $59 fee, and the opportunity was lost – most likely to the next guy on the ads.

Any sales opportunity like this should have been addressed with a free estimate or consultation. To lose a $10k opportunity over $59 is ridiculous. In this scenario, the $59 fee was a qualifier used to block out a price-sensitive time waster, and it was used incorrectly. I guarantee this happens every day in your market.

So just book the call, and let the professionals do the selling. If you lose the opportunity – so what? At least you got your foot in the door! If you're in a market where delivering good service is key, you can easily go in the opposite direction, advertise a free estimate, reduce your bids, and ride beneath someone who manages their business like this, and you'll make a killing.

Also, you want to be careful of advertising coupons in your market. They are historically ineffective, as they attract the most price-sensitive customers. Besides, if you start to advertise $25 OFF, your competitor will advertise $30 OFF, and the next guy will go to $49 OFF, so on and so forth. Let your competitors play this game, and instead of joining in, think of something that will differentiate you in the marketplace – something nobody else can do, or a bold promise you can deliver on. I'm talking about your *very best offer*.

11. **Monitor Competitor Ads Over the Long Haul:** It is very common for an advertisement to go lame. Many ads will do extremely well at first and then just go out to pasture and die. Market conditions are always liable to change, and the same language won't work every time.

   Luckily for our clients, we identify when this happens right away and take appropriate action. We routinely snapshot, track, and monitor our clients' competitive advertising landscapes. Your long-standing competitors probably don't have that degree of attention – so we track their ad changes to see if their manager is falling asleep at the wheel. In most cases, you'll find that your competitors are not split-testing their ads.

I'll use another one of my plumbing clients as an example: they were going up against a competitor in an aggressive market who called himself the #1 Plumber in the city, but he didn't do much to back it up. I knew this competitor had a chip on his shoulder, and his ego drove him to outbid the market by any means necessary. So instead of engaging in a bidding war, we decided to cut our bids down by 70% and completely retool our advertising approach. We introduced "5 Star Service & 50 Reviews To Prove It" into our ad strategy and backed it up with testimonials from places including Google Reviews, Yelp and many more. We've been doing it for over a year now. That same competitor still runs the same old ads, and we're absolutely killing it for our client.

Remember, if you are trying to manipulate or outsmart your prospects with slick ad copy or bait-and-switch methods, you are only going to attract the type of lead who falls for this trickery. You'll end up with a dumb-as-nails client who is most likely not qualified to buy from you in the first place. So keep it honest, build value, and if you offer a bold guarantee, prove it. The high quality prospects appreciate honestly and authority – that's why positioning yourself as the expert is so critical to winning the AdWords game.

12. **Take Advantage of Google "Throttling":** It's 2:00 in the afternoon, and you start to notice your competitors falling off in the search results. Their ads are no longer appearing. There is a good chance they have reached their daily budget, or they are coming very close. Most of your competitors are probably running standard campaigns and failing to protect themselves from click fraud, which means they are going to gas-out of budget before the end of the day. This is a great time for you to come in guns blazing and dominate your local search environment.

Riding into the battle later in the day when conditions are

less competitive will mean that you're spending way less than you would earlier to make the phone ring. And, since most of your good clients are employed or busy, you can craft an ad communicating that you are open for business through 8:00 PM. You'll be the only one available to chase down these leads.

A small change like this will help you capture the audience looking for your product or service right away. Clients expect to be serviced on their time. Remember, today's shoppers are conditioned to expect a certain level of instant gratification. It's important to treat them to service on-demand. If you take a look at the most successful business models in America, especially on the retail level, you'll find that a large part of their ads is about being available when their competitors are not – they do that because that's *what people want.* But you don't have to be a billion dollar retailer to *know your ideal customers* and operate at times that appeal to them.

So go ahead and take advantage of your competitors' budget strategy and enter into your local market when it makes the most sense. Be open to adapting and changing your work hours to accommodate these high value clients, customers, or patients.

13. **Take Advantage of Competitors who have "Feature Frenzy":** Google has plenty of conversion elements you can introduce to ad copy. We discussed these "ad extensions" earlier, so you know they include call extensions, location extensions, sitelinks and more. Leveraging these features in your sales copy appropriately can make your ads significantly more effective.

However, they can also be overused.

Sometimes you'll find a competitor who sets up *every one of these,* most likely as a result of an inexperienced PPC manager who thinks they'll get a better result. I can't count how many times I've seen a service contractor like an appliance repair, plumbing, electrical, or HVAC company advertise with location extensions despite this being an amateur mistake. Location extensions advertise your physical office address: 99% of the time in the residential service business, you are going to *the homeowner* and they're not coming to you, so why would you advertise your location?

It doesn't make any sense.

A location extension is perfect for a dentist, attorney, chiropractor, restaurant owner, et cetera – anyone with a physical brick and mortar office or storefront. However, they serve no purpose to companies that perform exclusively in-home jobs. In fact, if I'm a consumer living in City X and noticed in your ad copy you were located in City Y 5 miles away, I most likely would not call you, since I'm the type of guy looking for a local, in-my-city company to do the work. Even though you may have a technician who lives on my street, you'll be losing my call.

Another example of an often abused and misused feature is the call extension. Google provides you the ability to use their 800 number call extensions – however, I strongly advise against it. Why? Because you can't control the phone number that shows up in the ad. Instead, I would recommend securing your very own local numbers and using them in your call ad extensions. This will help you appear to be more relevant to the people living in the city or town you are marketing to. I understand that local numbers are hard to come by in some markets, but this is worth the search.

You should have a dedicated phone number for each different exchange in your local market. Stay away from using 800 numbers in your advertisements if at all possible. If you are working with an agency, make sure you know which lines they are using! All too often, they'll used recycled lines – I've seen it happen many times. For example, I've seen ad copy in Boston for a local business where they were using New York exchanges...and if you know anything about Boston, you know we can't stand Yankees fans. Be smart about how your location and phone number appear.

14. **Keyword Organization and Fine Tuning Adgroups:** Earlier, we discussed the importance of knowing your Google Quality Score. Part of running a successful Google AdWords program is achieving the best possible Quality Score you can manage. This

process involves reorganizing, retooling, and re-categorizing (or, as we call it, "bucketing") your keywords into contained adgroups within your campaign setup. One of the biggest mistakes people make in their AdWords campaigns is incorrectly organizing their keywords into comparable buckets.

In a perfect world, each of your adgroups would start with less than a dozen keywords optimized with ad copy and pointed to a landing page. But in reality, you probably won't have this degree of precision from the get-go. Still, optimization starts with having every keyword in its place, so be ready to test and adjust your initial adgroups and strategy.

For example, let's assume you are a chiropractor. Here are just a handful of keywords that may be relevant to your campaign:

- Back pain relief
- Degenerative disc disease
- Spinal stenosis
- Scoliosis
- Herniated disc
- Non surgical back pain treatments
- Back pain treatment
- Back pain symptoms
- Back pain help
- Back pain elimination

Organizing an adgroup is like putting together a puzzle: you need to inspect each keyword to find the pieces that fit together. What are the similar terms in this exercise? There are several Back Pain terms, so you could easily bucket them into an adgroup like the one below:

- Back pain relief
- Non surgical back pain treatments
- Back pain treatment
- Back pain symptoms
- Back pain help
- Back pain elimination

Now, over time (and with the right historical data), you may find that the term "*non-surgical back pain treatments*" has delivered to you the highest quality leads in the largest volume. You might also learn (since this is a long-tail keyword), that you can drive down your click costs with a lower bid and get the same result. You may even consider isolating this specific keyword in an adgroup all on its own with a new dedicated landing page. All of this is possible because you did the initial work that helped you be organized and clearly see your results.

At the end of the day, keyword and adgroup optimization is a gradual refinement process. It takes patience, data and time but the optimal Google AdWords result is worth the wait.

15. **Use Long-Tail Keywords:** The main reason that long-tail keywords are important is that they are cheaper – they allow you to target your highest quality leads at the lowest possible cost. But there are other reasons to look into long-tail keyword strategies as well.

With the emergence of mobile devices, people are assisted in finding information through artificial intelligence programs like Siri, and we've just started to see the power of this technology. You can press the button on your iPhone and ask Siri "find me the closest auto repair shop." Google offers the very same voice activated technology on Android mobile device browsers.

If you ever dig into the keywords that you've paid for in the past, you will see real evidence of voice-operated search. This under-the-radar game-changer has been impacting AdWords for years. It also represents a solid opportunity to think of phrases you would use to find your product or service. In my experience, most of your competitors won't be thinking outside the box like this – they are fighting for very direct and obvious terms like *auto repair CITY* or *CITY auto repair.* A simple long tail keyword could be *find me an auto repair shop in CITY.*

Now, you will not get a ton of traffic from this term, but over time it adds up – especially since the traffic you do get will be immediately interested in your service. As I said, the benefit of a long tail keyword is that it is very possible for you to bid very low, sometimes pennies on the dollar, and still have your ad appear and consistently convert for this type of phrase.

16. **Ad Copy Fine Tuning:** Another best practice is to constantly test – and through testing improve – the click-through rates on your ads. As seen in an earlier example in the "Ad Copy" chapter, a simple 1% improvement in CTR can change the entire performance dynamic of a campaign! That's why it is so important to test slight variations of your ad copy. In this case, I'm talking about text ads in the search network.

To be perfectly honest, you don't get much real estate. In fact, Google gives you less than 130 characters to build out an ad. Here are the limits:

Headline: Max Length 25 characters

Description Line 1: Max Length 35 characters

Description Line 2: Max Length 35 characters

Display URL: 35 characters

Here are some rules I follow when implementing ad copy:

- **Always work the keyword into the headline to start** – This step is simply mandatory for a good Quality Score and conversion.

- **Consider alternate URLs** – Most of your competitors will treat the display URL as just a website placeholder, but you can get creative by purchasing a domain with an action statement. For instance if you own Bob's Roof Repair, you can go out and purchase CallBobsRoofRepair. com. This changes the dynamic of how you leverage that space.

- **Be Straightforward and Concise** – Don't try to squeeze in too much information. Here's a random search I conducted looking for a New Orleans Roofer. Take a look at this ad:

Roofing Contractor
www.fordroofingservice.com/ ▾
Roofing, Siding, Patio covers
Free estimates, Fully Insured

I typed in roofer in the search box, and this ad includes siding and patio covers. That's inefficient marketing right there.

Google AdWords is all about targeting your consumer with laser-focus. What's the point of all the flexibility Google AdWords gives you if you're trying to fit your entire business model into a space the size of a postage stamp? So if you offer multiple services or sell a number of products, only focus your ad to include the actual product or service that the searcher is looking for.

These guys in New Orleans really made it easy for me. Here are a few more from the same search. Let's examine these ads:

Houma Roofers
www.roofingcontractoria.net/ ▾
Reliable Roofing Company. Call our
Roofer for an Estimate.

Brads Roofing
plus.google.com/RoofingContractor ▾
Certified Master **Roofers** since 1997
roof repairs and whole roofs

Let's tear apart urgency in the ad copy: it's pretty clear there isn't any. I guarantee if the top advertiser worked in the word "Today" after "Estimate", he would increase his CTR. The bottom advertiser doesn't have a call-to-action or any benefits-driven copy.

Let's rewrite the ad copy, and I'll walk you through the structure.

> *Roofer Available Today*
> *Call Now for Same Day Repair & Free*
> *Estimate. Ask About Lifetime Pledge*
> *CallStevesRoofing.com*

What made my version different?

- In my first line, I've accomplished three things with "Roofer Available Today": I have worked in my keyword, created urgency, and advertised instant availability with the word today.

- In the next line, I worked in *"Call Now for Same Day Repair."* Here I am disqualifying people who do not have an urgent need for a repair and are just shopping around for a roofer. I want to capture my repair audience, because these are people with an immediate need. Something just came through their roof, and they need service *today*. I'm targeting the "Give It To Me Now" customer profile.

- I worked in *"Free Estimate"* to take away any risk associated with the purchase, which almost guarantees me a foot in the door when the prospect calls.

- The *"Ask About Lifetime Pledge"* line builds trust and differentiates you in the market place. It also does one more thing: it reinforces the word "call" and influences the dynamic so that when people *do* pick up the phone, they'll be less likely to be combative. They might actually ask about the lifetime pledge, giving you extra leverage. NOTE: I would have preferred the word "promise" or "guarantee," but I ran out of runway with Google's space restrictions, so I had to get creative. To make effective sales copy, you need to involve your imagination.

Now you can pick a section of the ad and run a split-test to see which one gives you the better result. Normally, I'd like to start off with testing either my hook or close – in this example, we'll do the latter, the*"Ask About Lifetime Pledge"* line. Here's what I'd split-test it against:

> *Roofer Available Today*
> *Call Now for Same Day Repair & Free*
> *Estimate. Ask For Our References.*
> *CallStevesRoofing.com*

I am frequently asked, "How often should I split-test my ad copy, and when is the appropriate time to give up on an ad?" My rule of thumb is 100 impressions. If I can't get a 1% click-through rate on 100 impressions, I know I need to try something else. Once I start getting a good result, let's say 3% or better, I'll split-test an ad approximately every 500 impressions.

You want to be careful of knee jerking your ad copy or bailing on it without decent data. First, you need to give it time to ramp up with Google: it needs to pass their sniff test and then undergo the Google Quality Score evaluation or approval process. If you change your ads daily trying to get a quick result, you will most likely fail at producing that killer ad you're striving for.

17. **Advertising to People in Different Languages:** There are people in your market searching for your products and services who may speak perfect English but prefer to search in a completely different language. Google provides you with the ability to target people by language. For example, if you would like to target Spanish-speaking customers, you can launch an AdWords campaign with Spanish keywords and ads. Those ads will be served to Spanish-speaking prospects who have configured their Google interface language settings.

18. **Target by Device:** Let's say you own a tow truck company. Clearly, the best opportunities to capture and convert prospects would be when their vehicle breaks down. If they don't have AAA, they will most likely reach for their smartphones and search for a towing company. Similarly, if you own a drain cleaning company, your best prospect may be someone who has a backed up drain in their basement or first floor slab. There's a good chance that prospect is also taking their smartphone with them to the source of the problem.

Google provides you the ability to actually be very precise in your bid and ad strategies when it comes to devices. You can increase your mobile bids in a given adgroup, enhancing your chances to capture the audience that uses their phones as a search tool. It is very possible to see your ads positioned in the 5th or 6th slot on a desktop but increase your mobile bids so you are number one for those types of situations. This is just another example of a flexible tool Google provides to help you reach the people you'd like to target.

19. **Blocking Locations:** Let's say you own a handyman business in Fort Myers, Florida. You can very easily setup your ads so they are showing up in, let's say, a 5 mile radius of Fort Myers. Assuming you worked the keyword "Fort Myers Handyman" into your campaign, it is very possible that someone who owns a vacation home in New York and types in Fort Myers Handyman

will see your ad – unless, of course, you don't allow them to by blocking that location. Within the Google Campaign setup interface, you can omit locations so that your ad will NOT show up unnecessarily for overlapping city names on a given search term.

20. **Search and Display Networks:** Did you know that, when you first establish a campaign, Google will automatically submit your ads to their entire search network unless you tell them otherwise? The search network is Google's collective list of publishers for whom your ads will appear outside of the Google search results. They include more minor search engines such as AOL. You may see your ads in Gmail, on YouTube, and on other publisher sites. The Display Network was formerly known as the Content Network. Currently, it is made up of more than a million websites, applications, and videos. The Display Network is a common place for product-based companies, specifically e-commerce companies, to show up.

Here's a screenshot of a combined Google search and display result for the term: "Canon Powershot." In this image, you can see both text ads and display ads running side by side.

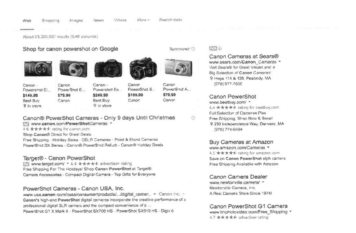

I recommend that, when you are first starting out – before you understand your core metrics of success – that you limit your exposure to just Google Search. Go ahead and turn off the entire search network. We can reconsider it later on in the process, but for now it just complicates matters unnecessarily. The same holds true for the Microsoft Network – Bing and Yahoo. Master Google first, then grow your strategy by tracking the right performance metrics throughout.

21. **Remarketing**: Everybody lives a busy life these days. Sometimes, a person will have a free moment at work and decide to do a little research about a purchase they've been thinking about – they might even click on an ad or two in the process. When work starts back up again, however, they completely move on and forget what they just saw. It's a very common situation for a prospect to be casually surfing the web, be interested enough in your business to follow one of your ads, but then become distracted by something else and never actually enter your sales funnel. Particularly for large ticket items, it can be extremely frustrating to have these clicks that aren't generating calls. But sometimes people are just too busy to remember you, right?

Well, with Google AdWords Remarketing, you can personally remind them. When a prospect visits your website, remarketing lets us drop a cookie on their browser that remembers what they've seen. Then, later on, when the same prospect is looking for highlights on ESPN.com or watching the news at CNN's website, your ads appear in designated spaces on the page. Your branding follows the prospects to increase your lead capture and strengthen your conversion for those long-term sells!

Let's say, for example, that you're a jewelry retailer. There's a guy looking to buy his wife a nice diamond necklace. He looks up jewelry retailers near him and comes across your ad, as well as a number of others. He visits your site and even finds your location. But later on, he becomes so wrapped up in work, commuting, and unwinding at home that he forgets he had wanted the necklace. That's a lost lead, right?

Maybe for your competitors. But if you have remarketing, you can remind him during his later web surfing with banner ads that appear at the top and sides of the screen. This brings your company and his intended purchase back to his mind – heck, if it's his anniversary, he'll thank you!

Remarketing on Google AdWords isn't designed to get you a higher click volume. It's designed to increase your web presence, reinforce your brand legitimacy, and reintroduce your company to lost opportunities. Savvy AdWords managers will be using this program for their longer sales funnels and designing polished, professional-looking banner ads to represent their business.

So there you have it: 21 proven-to-work strategies and best practices for managing any AdWords account.

I'd like to add one more item to the list, though. It's a best practice I've mentioned before, but I feel that it could always use repeating: one of the most critical components of having successful AdWords campaigns is having the right relationship with your PPC manager. Of course, at this point, you have a much better understanding of what you should be expecting, and you know the questions that you should ask before signing any contract. But what does it look like on the PPC managers end? In the next and final section, I want to take a little time to discuss exactly that.

8.3 - A Day in the Life of The Professional PPC Manager

As I've mentioned throughout the book, Google AdWords management requires some muscle and mental fortitude. It's 50% strategy, 40% hands-on, grind-it-out, grunt-effort, elbow-grease, et cetera, and 10% emotional roller coaster. For a PPC manager, it's kind of like being a stock broker – but in a quiet, geeky sort of way, if that makes any sense. Like *Wolf of Wall Street*, but without quite as much stripping, Quaaludes, drunk driving, public nudity, failed marriages – you know what, maybe it's not that much like *Wolf on Wall Street*. But it's certainly a wild time.

When you walk into my PPC operations center, you'll notice that each PPC manager has a quad monitor setup. Here's what's on each monitor:

The top left hand monitor provides a real-time data feed of our in-house software solution, ClickOptix, which I've been telling you about. This software will be performing a function we invented that we like to call "Click Accounting." It shows the PPC managers all of the clicks that are happening on each of the accounts they manage. They are able to see if the clicks were fraud, which keywords were used to trigger the click, and which ad was served in addition to which landing page the prospective client visited. The technology is able to tell the PPC manager if the click resulted in a conversion or phone call. Clicks that did not result in a phone call are researched, and the PPC manager begins the optimization and refinement process for that specific keyword, ad copy, and landing page. All of this happens minutes after a click takes place. This real-time daily management allows us to instantly make improvements on our client account performance.

- The top right hand side of the PPC manager's set up shows the calls coming into our clients' organizations in real-time. They are able to monitor call performance, make tweaks to negative keywords, and split-test ad copy in order to improve lead quality.

- The bottom two screens are used to work directly inside the Google AdWords interface using both Google AdWords and the Google AdWords editor.

- Above the PPC manager, the call audio is being played in the background. As soon as a call is completed from one of our client accounts, it goes into a queue and plays throughout the floor, that way if a PPC manager is not listening independently at his workstation, he is still getting fallback audio of calls into every organization we manage.

- In the PPC operations center, we have a large flat-screen that scrolls all of our clients performance data in a "stock ticker/heart monitor" fashion. What's neat about this is that we are able to identify and work on changes to market conditions in real-time. The program, which is called Click Scorecard, documents all of our clients' real-time performance data including budget, spend, cost per click, cost per call, and conversion. It benchmarks these metrics against their historical performance and others in their industry. If for any reason their numbers fall outside of our standard, a team is assigned to the account right away to bring the numbers back to alignment.

- On another flat-screen, we manage all systems related to server performance. We are able to manage and optimize landing page performance and ensure all of our systems are in working order.

When we bring on a client, we offer world-class deliverables and manage their account daily. Our systems provide our PPC managers with crystal clear transparency along with black and white practical data to drive down costs and optimize performance.

Chapter 8 Survivor's Summary

For the final chapter of the *Survival Guide*, our top priority was to think of ways you can outsmart your competitors and gain control of your local market. To do this, Steve guided you through the 21 strategies he uses to make his own clients successful using Google AdWords. This included his #1 rule of PPC: the $53,000 to One rule of time management. You can now use these serviceable techniques to make your own AdWords account start performing! To complete the chapter, Steve gave a detailed account of what a single day in the life of a PPC manager looks like. You heard Steve's description of his team's setup, as well as how ClickOptix functions in his office to track and optimize performance.

Your takeaways from this chapter should be what to expect in your first 90 days and what you can do to manage a successful long-term AdWords account.

Test Your Survival Skills: *(Find answers on page 190)*

1. You should consider looking into getting a _____ for your branding in order to prevent others in your market from running aggressive competitor campaigns.

2. Google AdWords copy has restrictive dimensions: you only have _____ characters to work with for your headline and _____ for your display URL.

3. If you can't get a 1% click-through rate on _____ impressions, you should try new ad copy.

Conclusion

Congratulations: you've reached the end of my *Google AdWords Survival Guide*.

However, you're not yet at the end of what this book can offer you. My *Survival Guide* is designed so that you can take it with you on all of your AdWords adventures. When you're lost in the jungle of PPC jargon, go to the "AdWords Lexicon" to help you find your way. When your monthly budget is bleeding, reach for the "First Aid Kit" on your utility belt. When you're drowning, just grab hold of your lifesaver!

The end of each chapter contains a list of additional assets available to you through my website. The world of Google AdWords is too vast to fit in one book – so this *Survival Guide* is also a springboard to finding other crucial resources to help you generate more leads.

Use the "Survivor's Summaries" to find materials that are relevant to your specific queries. The guide is structured linearly: it starts by breaking away from AdWords strategies that aren't working (LOST AT SEA), then moves into building a smarter foundation for success (THE 3 SURVIVAL NECESSITIES), and from there transitions into the techniques and best practices that will help you thrive (IT'S GO TIME).

Since this is the conclusion, I'll take this opportunity to summarize the formula for AdWords success. You'll recognize these themes from the book because they have been the underlying truths backing everything I've said. These three simple rules should be your gut reactions to Google AdWords scenarios as you set out to try again. They are the core principles of any successful campaign.

The 3 Most Important AdWords Survival Instincts

- **Ensure Live Management of Your Account** –Always have a human in control of your AdWords account.

  Whether you want to find a PPC manager who can guide you (since we can't all invest the time it takes to be survival experts) or if you want to take on Google AdWords marketing on your own, make sure that your business's campaigns aren't just trapped on an algorithm with hundreds of others. As a real-time marketing tool, AdWords is time-intensive, and it loses its effectiveness when you aren't giving it the attention it needs.

You should have a trustworthy point-of-contact whom you can regularly speak to without having to re-explain your business all over again. Remember, communication is key.

✪ **Take a Conversion-Based Approach** – Measure your AdWords account's performance by standards that directly affect ROI: the single most important metric to keep track of is not impressions or click-through-rates but *conversion*, the percentage of ad clicks that are becoming leads.

High conversion should be the primary goal of your ads. Build campaigns that entice, sales copy that persuades, and landing pages that are optimized to make people call.

Don't be suckered in by PPC managers who only tell you traffic numbers or claim to generate leads without showing you where they come from. Use a conversion-based approach and demand total transparency. It's the only way to get your budget's worth.

✪ **Differentiate Yourself in Your Market** – When you see your competitors heading in one direction, go the other way. Since this is a *Survival Guide*, let's think of it in animal terms.

Lemmings move in packs, and they aren't very bright. They scare easily, so they usually just take the path of least resistance and follow it to its end. When they get to a resource, there isn't much of it to go around. They often fall off cliffs in their mass migrations when the leader takes a dive.

On the other hand, you've got the lynx: a big cat and a natural predator. The lynx hunts alone, and it takes on big game when it can. It's at the top of its food chain, and it eats rodents like the lemming for breakfast.

Be a lynx, not a lemming: confront your market on your own terms. Don't just run the same deals and try to beat your competitors on pricing – be smart about your ad copy and split-test. There's only strength in numbers if you're all on the same team.

Of course, it's easier said than done – but I've been saying that all along. Optimizing Google AdWords properly is a process that takes time, effort, and experience, not to mention the initial cost of technology and trial investment. The road to Google AdWords success is not the path of least resistance, and all of your marketing survival skills are going to be put to the test.

But here's why it's worth it: your potential customers are no longer going to the yellow pages when they need service. They are no longer thumbing through catalogues for products, and they are no longer responding as strongly to direct mailings. When a consumer needs a professional's help, they go to the internet. Through Google, they can find reviews of the businesses in their area, the phone numbers of companies to call, promotions to take advantage of, and even downloadable assets to help in their search. That's why Google has over a trillion unique visitors every year. With Google AdWords, you don't just get the widest audience of any marketing medium possible – you get opportunities to directly target and communicate with your specific demographic. You get to send out ads and have them visible immediately, and you get to pay an adjustable amount based on how many people show interest in your advertisement.

This is the future of advertising. Google AdWords presents marketing capabilities unlike any other for local companies.

Small and medium businesses stand to profit immensely from the features AdWords makes available to them – features like premier ad placement, remarketing for lead capture, targeting by search terms, and ad extensions for maximum user-efficiency. The problem is that too many AdWords users don't even know where to begin. They wind up being taken advantage of by publicly traded corporations that specialize in sales but have no real interest in managing accounts. They plan their budgets incorrectly because they don't understand how the system works, and they aren't aware of how to track their metrics or their return on investment.

A little while back, that was you.

Well, now is your chance to be in control of your own destiny. This *Survival Guide* will help you capitalize on all of the resources at your disposal. I'm even offering you some new assets that the people who don't have this book don't have access to. You now have everything you need to make your internet marketing strong with PPC campaigns that get results.

Keep the *Google AdWords Survival Guide* at your side, and keep your head above water. Use these proven techniques for sales funnel construction and lead generation, and pretty soon you'll be a marketing survival expert yourself. And most of all, use your resources. I've taught you what you need to know – now take the helm!

Google AdWords is the tool that's going to help you widen your customer base and grow your business to the next level. Congrats again on making it this far – I look forward to seeing you survive and thrive in the internet marketing wild.

BONUS RESOURCES FOR THE GOOGLE ADWORDS SURVIVAL GUIDE

Gain access to over $805 worth of money making Google AdWords tools, step-by-step blueprints, and online training.

Discover how you can outsmart your competitors, prevent bleeding budgets, and grow your business with the power of Google AdWords when you join Pay-Per-Click Prosperity – the place for better Google AdWords advertising performance.

Here You'll Gain Access To:

- **Steve's AdWords Survival Blueprint ($29 value):** This one pager will be your best friend when you are attempting to navigate the waters of Google AdWords. It includes Google AdWords vocabulary, The Anatomy of a winning Google AdWords campaign and The Basic Survival Rules in Making Google AdWords work for you.

- **How To Hire a Google AdWords Advertising Manager Worksheet ($97 value):** This comprehensive worksheet includes the 21 essential interview questions you need to ask AdWords manager candidates to see if they are qualified to manage your precious advertising budget.

- **5 Step-By-Step Ways To Capture More Opportunities Using The Right Technology Webinar ($297 value):** Register now and watch this pre-recorded webinar on-demand. *Setting The Foundation For Google AdWords Success.* Watching this webinar will give you a clear picture and understanding into how wasted advertising spend can be easily be avoided, how you'll generate more leads and how you can implement a competitive edge that will take your competitors by complete surprise.

- **Steve's Ad Copy Survival Blueprint ($97 value):** This is the actual tool Steve uses with clients to develop a go-to market strategy for each and every single campaign he manages. This tool will make sure you don't miss a thing when you begin to craft your ad copy for Google AdWords.

- **Ad Copy Worksheet ($97 value):** This simple and powerful one page worksheet gives you the ability to simulate and test your ad copy. It will tell you exactly how many characters you can fit into your ad. In addition it will provide you with an example on how it will appear on Google's search results page.

- **Steve's Landing Page Survival Cheat Sheet ($29 value):** This guide provides you with all of the built-in best practices you should incorporate into your landing pages. Following these 10 essential landing page tips will keep your pages converting again and again.

- **3 Legged Stool of AdWords Success Worksheet ($47 value):** Built with more than 20 business metrics, this simple and easy tool will help you figure out how many leads your organization needs and how much you should budget for when launching a Google AdWords campaign. You will see directly how slight improvements in PPC management, call center management and sales management can impact revenue with this smart tool.

- **The Pay-Per-Click Scorecard ($97 value):** This powerful management template gives you the ability to measure and track the 14 key performance metrics that impact your Google AdWords return on investment. You'll be able to track all of your core AdWords, call center and revenue performance and tie it back to your monthly budget. This tool allows you to collect data month over month so you can keep a pulse on your month-over-month averages.

- **Free 30-Minute Review of your Google AdWords Account** Along with action items you can take to make immediate improvements with an experienced PPC lead generation and conversion specialist on Steve's team.

- **Free 30-Day Trial to ClickOptix Conversion Optimization and Reporting Software:** Never feel lost again with access to our real-time business reporting software – ClickOptix. You'll have up-to-the-minute access to the health, well-being, and critical reporting metrics that make your phone ring. View clicks, conversion rates, calls, top performing keywords, click fraud and much more.

- **Monthly Newsletter:** Stay up-to-date with changes, news and events and receive the monthly Pay-Per-Click Prosperity Client-Only Newsletter.

- **Weekly Live Group Coaching & Training Sessions** with Steve Teneriello and his team.

- **Access to Ready To Launch Campaigns:** Complete with landing pages, sales copy, graphics, and keywords these step-by-step campaign blueprints are available to help you drastically increase lead conversion.

Gain Access to these Bonus Resources, Tools and Training Today by Joining Pay-Per-Click Prosperity.

Get Started and Visit: www.payperclickprosperity.com

About The Author

Steve Teneriello

Google AdWords Lead Generation and Conversion Specialist

Steve Teneriello is a professional lead generation and conversion specialist. He manages Google AdWords pay-per-click accounts for local businesses across the nation. For more than a decade, he has dedicated his career to making small businesses successful with internet marketing, which has resulted in him generating well over 1 million leads for his clients in that time. He currently resides in Amesbury, Massachusetts with his wife, Allison, and his daughter, Madeline Rose.

Better Pay-Per-Click Performance Guaranteed™

Learn More At:
steveten.com

Steve Speaks at Your Business Event!
Attend a Google AdWords Survival Seminar

Every year, tens of thousands of local business owners experience the frustration of having a Google AdWords account that doesn't deliver returns. Month over month, they feel like they're wasting money on advertising that isn't generating leads or growing their business, and their PPC manager isn't doing anything to fix the problem – but it doesn't have to be that way!

With more than one million leads under his belt and over a decade of experience managing advertising budgets both large and small, local lead generation and conversion expert Steve Teneriello walks you through step-by-step proven strategies to outsmart your competitors, put an end to bleeding budgets once and for all, and quickly attract new customers, clients, or patients with The Google AdWords Survival Seminar.

In this Seminar, Teneriello Covers:

- How to Reach your Very Best Customers, Clients or Patients Starting Today.

- How to Prevent Being Eaten Alive by PPC Scammers, Scoundrels & Fraudsters.

- The 6 Ways to Increase Lead Volume That your PPC Manager Doesn't Want you to Know About.

- How to Uncover Your Prospects Pain and Turn Them Into new Customers, Clients or Patients Following These 10 Killer Ad Copy Rules.

- The 5 Secret Ingredients in Turning Clicks into Dollars.

- 7 Common Google AdWords Budget Bleeders and How to Fix Them.

- A Lesson in Google Math They Didn't Teach You in School.

- 21 Proven AdWords Strategies to Outsmart Your Competitors & Get More For Less.

To attend a seminar, go to: steveten.com/seminars

How To Reach Us

Author and Expert Steve Teneriello Can Help You Get Returns on Your PPC wherever you are!

If you enjoyed this book and would like more information, you can go to steveten.com to learn more about and request any of the following services:

- **Consulting** – Learn about lead generation from the best in the business. Steve and his team are available to contact for advice on lead generation and PPC marketing. You can discuss strategy with the experts and even perform one-on-one quality reviews of your campaigns.

- **ClickOptix Technology** – Find demonstrations of what ClickOptix looks like and what it can do for your business. This proprietary software is the latest in performance tracking and conversion optimization, and it's only available through Steve and his team.

- **Management** – Become one of Steve's successful clients! Steve has been managing PPC for years, and his peerless techniques have generated over one million leads for local businesses. You'll have access to all the technology, transparency, and guaranteed results you need to make your Google AdWords account a success when you work with the local experts.

- **Speaking and Seminars** – Request for author Steve Teneriello to speak at your business event! You can schedule your own seminar through speaking@steveten.com.

For volume discounts on The Google AdWords Survival Guide as well as all other services, go to steveten.com today.

[1] Internet Live Search. *Google Search Statistics*. 2014. http://www.internetlivestats.com/google-search-statistics/ (accessed 10 Nov 2014).

[2] Moz. *Google Algorithm Change History*. 2014. http://moz.com/google-algorithm-change. (accessed 4 Nov 2014).

[3] AdGooRoo. *AdWords Cost Per Click Rises 26% Between 2012 and 2014*. 2014. http://moz.com/google-algorithm-change (accessed 4 Nov 2014).

[4] PewResearch Internet Project. *Mobile Technology Fact Sheet*. 2014. http://www.pewinternet.org/fact-sheets/mobile-technology-fact-sheet/. (accessed 6 Nov 2014).

[5] Neilson, Google. *Mobile Search Moments*. 2013. https://www.thinkwithgoogle.com/research-studies/creating-moments-that-matter.html. (accessed 6 Nov 2014).

[6] Greg Sterling. Source: *Google Ending Reseller Program (For Now)*. 2010. http://searchengineland.com/sources-google-terminating-adwords-reseller-program-for-now-38955. (accessed 7 Nov 2014).

[7] Christ Silver Smith. *Google Announces New Reseller Program*. 2010. http://searchengineland.com/google-announces-new-reseller-program-50964. (accessed 7 Nov 2014).

[8] Christopher Heine. *AdWords Resellers Say Google Plans to Stop Huge Mark-Ups on SMBs*. 2010. http://www.clickz.com/clickz/news/1716656/adwords-resellers-say-google-plans-stop-huge-mark-ups-smbs. (accessed 7 Nov 2014).

[9] Ginny Marvin. *Agencies Take Note: Google Third-Party Policy Changes Coming Nov. 2014*. 2014. http://searchengineland.com/agencies-take-note-google-third-party-policy-changes-coming-nov-2014-206099. (accessed 1 Nov 2014).

[10] Google. *GOOGLE ADWORDS RESELLER AGREEMENT*. 2011. http://www.sec.gov/Archives/edgar/data/1297336/000119312511141662/dex102.htm. (accessed 5 Nov 2014).

[11] MarketWatch. *ReachLocal Reports Fourth Quarter Full Year 2014 Results*. 2014. http://www.marketwatch.com/story/reachlocal-reports-fourth-quarter-and-full-year-2013-results-2014-02-11. (accessed 6 Nov 2014).

[12] Greg Sterling. *Advertisers Paying Yearly Average of Over 18.5K to ReachLocal*. 2013. http://screenwerk.com/2013/11/05/advertisers-paying-yearly-average-of-18-5k-to-reachlocal/. (accessed 6 Nov 2014).

[13] Khadeesi Safdar and Angus Loten. *Small Businesses Search in Vain for Web-Ad Help*. 2014. http://www.wsj.com/articles/SB10001424052702304626304579505590654385248. (accessed 6 Nov 2014).

[14] Jessica E. Vascellaro. *Local Advertisers Still Skittish About Search*. 2009. http://blogs.wsj.com/digits/2009/06/08/local-advertisers-still-skittish-about-search/?mod=rss_WSJBlog?mod=. (accessed 4 Nov 2014).

[15] Khadeeja Safdar. *Small Business Web-Ads Aren't Reaching Targets*. 2014. http://www.wsj.com/articles/SB10001424052702304626304579505663515509926. (accessed 18 Dec 2014).

[16] Payam Zamani. *Why Companies Like Groupon, Yelp, and ReachLocal Aren't Dominating the Local Space*. 2013. http://www.forbes.com/sites/groupthink/2013/03/14/why-companies-like-groupon-yelp-and-reachlocal-arent-dominating-the-local-space/. (accessed 6 Nov 2014).

[17] Greg Sterling. *The Persistance of the SMB Churn Problem*. 2011. http://screenwerk.com/2011/06/06/the-persistence-of-the-smb-churn-problem/. (accessed 4 Nov 2014).

[18] Brian Bolan. *ReachLocal (NASDAQ: ROLC) Equity Research*. 2011. https://www.scribd.com/doc/61806412/ReachLocal-update-8-8-11. (accessed 4 Nov 2014).

[19] Yahoo Finance, from Zacks Investment Research. *ReachLocal Posts 3Q Loss*. 2014. http://finance.yahoo.com/news/reachlocal-posts-3q-loss-100402204.html. (accessed 4 Nov 2014).

[20] Sharon Rowlands. *It's Clear: Local Businesses Need More Transparency from Digital Marketing Providers*. 2014. http://www.forbes.com/sites/groupthink/2014/12/05/its-clear-local-businesses-need-more-transparency-from-digital-marketing-providers/. (accessed 4 Nov 2014).

21   Forbes. *America's Most Promising Companies*. 2014. http://www.forbes.com/companies/yodle/. (accessed 4 Nov 2014).

22   Deloitte. *Deloitte's 2011 Technology Fast 500 Ranking*. 2011. http://www.deloitte.com/assets/dcom-unitedstates/local%20assets/documents/tmt_us_tmt/us_tmt_2011fast500rankings_111411.pdf. (accessed 4 Nov 2014).

23   Peter Kravinsky. *SMBs, Search Packages, and Churn: Perspectives from Industry Leaders*. 2009. http://kelseygroup.openbox.net/twattach/DocLib_2150/ILM_ADV_0905.pdf. (accessed 4 Nov 2014).

24   Search Marketing Standard. *The World of Local Online Advertising: Court Cunningham of Yodle*. 2011. http://www.searchmarketingstandard.com/the-world-of-local-online-advertising-court-cunningham-of-yodle. (accessed 4 Nov 2014).

25   Greg Sterling. *Borrell Shines Light On "Local SEM" Churn*. 2009. http://searchengineland.com/borrell-shines-light-on-local-sem-churn-20627. (accessed 8 Nov 2014).

26   Greg Sterling. *What Are ReachLocal's Churn Numbers*. 2014. http://screenwerk.com/2014/04/12/what-are-reachlocals-churn-numbers/. (accessed 8 Nov 2014).

27   Thrive Analytics. *Press Releases*. 2013. http://www.thriveanalytics.com/Press%20Release-Advertiser%20Outlook%20Report.html. (accessed 8 Nov 2014).

28   Stephen Church and Andrea Tan. *Dex, Supermedia File for Bankruptcy to Complete Merger*. 2013. http://www.bloomberg.com/news/2013-03-18/dex-supermedia-file-for-bankruptcy-to-complete-merger.html. (accessed 4 Nov 2014).

29   Dex Media. *SuperMedia Awarded Google AdWords Premier SMB Partner Status*. 2012. http://www.dexmedia.com/news/google-adwords-premier-smb-partner/. (accessed 4 Nov 2014).

30   Greg Sterling. *US Yellow Pages Publishers Merge to Form Entity Focused on Local-Digital Advertising*. 2012. http://searchengineland.com/us-yellow-pages-publishers-merge-to-form-entity-focused-on-local-digital-advertising-131138. (accessed 4 Nov 2014).

31   Josh Janssen. *Yellow Pages Scam: The Google Partnership*. 2011. http://www.melbournegeek.com/2011/08/yellow-pages-scam/#.VJfS_MAAI. (accessed 4 Nov 2014).

32   Retailing Today. *Study: 81% research online before making big purchases*. 2013. http://www.retailingtoday.com/article/study-81-research-online-making-big-purchases. (accessed 10 Nov 2014).

33   Google and Ipsos MediaCT. *Google Small Business Pulse Check*. 2013. https://gabo-central.appspot.com/content/static_file/Google_SMB_PulseCheck%20Report_External%20(for%20PR)%20-%20Shortened.pdf?view=1. (accessed 10 Nov 2014).

34   Greg Sterling. *Survey: Only 6 Percent of SMBs Have Mobile Sites, 45% Don't Have Any at All*. 2014. http://marketingland.com/survey-online-6-percent-smbs-mobile-sites-45-percent-dont-site-73937. (accessed 10 Nov 2014).

35   Localpoint. *Mobile Industry Statistics*. 2013. http://digby.com/mobile-statistics/. (accessed 10 Nov 2014).

36   Ginny Marvin. *Mobile to Drive 50 Percent of Google Paid Search Clicks By End of 2015 [Study]*. 2014. http://searchengineland.com/smartphones-drive-50-percent-google-paid-search-clicks-end-2015-study-187013. (accessed 10 Nov 2014).

37   David Raab. *Marketing Automation's Unhappy Users: Trouble in Paradise?* 2013. http://customerexperiencematrix.blogspot.com/2013/10/marketing-automations-unhappy-users.html. (accessed 6 Nov 2014).

38   Dr. Peter J. Meyers. *Eye-Tracking Google SERPS - 5 tales of Pizza*. 2011. http://moz.com/blog/eyetracking-google-serps. (accessed 15 Nov 2014).

39   Creative Marketing & Design Solutions. *Where do most people click on Google?* 2013. http://www.cmdsonline.com/the-looking-glass/internet-marketing-services/ppc-management-company/where-do-most-people-click-on-google/. (accessed 15 Nov 2014).

40   Tim Shivers. *Traffic From Google SERPs Has Changed: Heat Maps Study*. 2014. http://www.capturecommerce.com/blog/business/traffic-google-serps-changed-heat-maps-study/. (accessed 15 Nov 2014).

41   Salesforce Marketing Cloud. *2014 Mobile Behavior Report*. 2014. http://www.exacttarget.com/sites/exacttarget/files/deliverables/etmc-2014mobilebehaviorreport.pdf. (accessed 6 Nov 2014).

Test Your Survival Skills:
Survivor's Summary Answers

Chapter 1
1. impressions
2. 3.5 billion/40,000
3. real-time

Chapter 2
1. 26
2. performance metrics
3. 30-60
4. 3 month

Chapter 3
1. 50
2. click fraud

Chapter 4
1. "Researcher"
2. risk-reversal offers
3. Quality Score
4. call extension

Chapter 5
1. more
2. naked
3. responsive
4. call-to-action

Chapter 6
1. Standard/ Accelerated
2. negative keyword

Chapter 7
1. average cost of client acquisition/ client's LTV
2. $33.33
3. conversion
4. booking rate
5. average transaction size

Chapter 8
1. trademark
2. 25/35
3. 100

17122016R10110

Made in the USA
Middletown, DE
07 January 2015